THE
QUEEN
MUM

Her first 100 years

THE Sun

THE QUEEN MUM
Her first 100 years

Arthur Edwards
& Charles Rae

HarperCollinsPublishers

First published in 2000
By HarperCollins*Publishers*
77–85 Fulham Palace Road
London W6 8JB

Printed and bound in Britain by Bath Press Colourbooks

British Cataloguing in Publication Data
A catalogue record for this book is available from the British Library
ISBN 0-00-710384-0

THE AUTHORS:

ARTHUR EDWARDS has worked as a *Sun* photographer since 1974 and recently celebrated 25 years service. Born in Epping, Essex, he has been taking pictures of the royal family since 1977 and is a well known face to the royals. Happily married to Ann since 1961, they have three children: John and Paul, who both work for *The Sun;* and Annmarie. They also have two grandchildren, Lucy and Katy.

CHARLES RAE is *The Sun*'s Royal Correspondent and has been a journalist for more than 30 years. He has worked for *The Sun*, first covering labour news and now the royals. He left *The Sun* to work for *Today* newspaper for 6 years where he started covering the royals, before returning to *The Sun*. Born in Glasgow, Scotland, he is happily married to Jill and they have two children Robert and Fiona.

ACKNOWLEDGEMENTS

The authors would like to acknowledge the assistance of Jane Reed, Colin Mackenzie, Edward Whitaker, Ken Lennox, Judy Wade, Hilary Scase, Peter Simpson, Marc Giddings, Paul Edwards, Tom Petrie, Tony Eyles, James Clench, Alison Croose, Chris Hockley, and offer special thanks to Chris Whalley and staff at News International Reference and picture libraries and a number of others who cannot be named for obvious reasons. A special thank you also to editor Philip Parker for keeping us on the straight and narrow and insisting that we met his deadlines, to Colin Brown for his fantastic book design, and to Becky Goddard and Katy Lygoe for their able and cheerful job in co-ordinating the project.

Contents

THE QUEEN MUM'S 100 YEARS

1900   The Queen Mother is born in the same month the British get their first taste of Coca Cola.

1910   Edward VII dies of pneumonia and is buried in the family vault at St George's Chapel. George V succeeds him.

1911   King George V is crowned at Westminster Abbey.

1923   Bertie and Elizabeth are married at Westminster Abbey.

1926   The Duchess of York gives birth to her first child Elizabeth Alexandra Mary, the future queen.

1928   Royal doctors tend the King in Buckingham Palace. He is suffering from fever and lung congestion.

1930   Princess Margaret Rose is born – a sister for Princess Elizabeth.

1935   May – King George and Queen Mary celebrate their silver jubilee. Four generations of the royal family pack into St Paul's.

1936   King George V dies and is buried at Windsor. He is succeeded by King Edward VIII.
King Edward VIII abdicates, plunging Britain into constitutional crisis. He is to marry American divorcee Wallis Simpson. Succeeding him is Prince Albert, who becomes King George VI. It is a pivotal moment in the 36-year-old Queen Mum's life, as she becomes Queen Elizabeth.

1937   May – King George VI and Queen Elizabeth are crowned at Westminster Abbey. The Queen receives a circlet of diamonds including the prestigious Koh-i-noor. Princess Elizabeth and Princess Margaret Rose sit between Queen Mary and her daughter, the Princess Royal.
June – The Duke of Windsor, formerly King Edward VIII, is married to Wallis Simpson.
Duke and Duchess of Windsor meet with Hitler in Germany.

1938   The King opens the Empire Exhibition in Glasgow. Queen Elizabeth is presented with the Badge of the Order of the Thistle, Scotland's highest order of chivalry.

1939   June – The King and Queen visit the World Fair in New York. They get a rapturous welcome from the Americans.

1940   Sep – London is under fire as Luftwaffe bombs drop on the East End. The King and Queen are in Buckingham Palace when it is hit.

1 9 4 7	Princess Elizabeth and Lt. Philip Mountbatten are married at Westminster Abbey.
1 9 4 8	Princess Elizabeth gives birth to a son Charles Philip Arthur George.
1 9 5 0	Princess Anne Elizabeth Alice Louise is born to Princess Elizabeth.
1 9 5 2	King George VI dies.
1 9 5 3	Queen Elizabeth II is crowned.
1 9 6 0	Prince Andrew is born. Princess Margaret and Tony Armstrong Jones are married.
1 9 6 4	Prince Edward is born.
1 9 6 9	Prince Charles is invested as Prince of Wales at Caernarvon Castle.

1 9 7 2	Duke of Windsor dies in Paris and his body is flown home and buried at Frogmore.
1 9 7 3	Princess Anne and Captain Mark Phillips marry at Westminster Abbey.
1 9 7 4	Attempted kidnap of Princess Anne in the Mall
1 9 7 5	US leaves Vietnam in humiliating rush. Spanish monarchy restored.
1 9 7 7	Birth of the Queen Mother's first grandchild Peter Phillips to Princess Anne
1 9 7 8	Princess Margaret and Lord Snowdon are divorced.
1 9 7 9	Earl Mountbatten is assassinated by an IRA bomb
1 9 8 1	Birth of Zara Phillips to Princess Anne. Marriage of Diana and Prince Charles
1 9 8 2	Birth of Prince William to Princess Diana.

1 9 8 4	Birth of Prince Harry, Princess Diana's second son.
1 9 8 6	Prince Andrew and Sarah Ferguson marry at Westminster and they are created the Duke and Duchess of York.
1 9 8 8	Birth of Princess Beatrice to the Duchess of York
1 9 9 2	Queen Elizabeth describes year as *annus horribilis* after fire ravages Windsor Castle. Divorce of Princess Anne and Mark Phillips. The Duke and Duchess of York separate, as do Prince Charles and Princess Diana. In December Princess Anne marries Commander Tim Laurence at Crathie church in Scotland.
1 9 9 4	Queen Mother's death is announced in a newsflash – it was wrongly transmitted in a rehearsal error.
1 9 9 6	Charles and Diana divorce. Andrew and Fergie Divorce
1 9 9 7	Diana, Princess of Wales, is killed in a car crash in Paris.

1 9 9 9	Prince Edward and Sophie Rhys-Jones marry at Windsor Charles and his lover Camilla Parker Bowles make their first public appearance together in 25 years after a party at the Ritz Hotel in London.
2 0 0 0	4th August – The Queen Mum turns 100.

ONE HUNDRED NOT OUT

Most people would have retired gracefully 35 or even 40 years ago, happy enough to enjoy a cuppa while watching Richard and Judy on the telly. But not Her Majesty Queen Elizabeth the Queen Mother ... the good old Queen Mum to a nation of admirers. Her sense of duty and her overwhelming desire to avoid disappointing the British people have made sure she is still at the very forefront of the Royal Family, carrying out ceremonies and appearing at functions despite her 100 incredible years on this Earth.

She really is, as the newspaper cliché goes, Britain's favourite gran – though of course she has long since been a great grandmother. To many she is the epitome of Britishness. Dignified. Calm in a crisis. Confident, witty and not a little loveable. Qualities that have earned her a unique place in the affections of her countrymen and women that is unlikely to be rivalled for many years to come.

> 'She has the extraordinary ability to bring happiness to other people's lives. And her own vitality and warmth is returned by those who she meets.'

This Sun book, by two Sun journalists who know the Queen Mum better than anyone beyond the perimeters of Buckingham Palace and Clarence House, will lift the veil of mystery that still surrounds her, offering a unique insight into the seismic events that have shaped her, and revealing what makes her laugh, what makes her angry – and what makes her cry.

Accompanied by a spectacular gallery of photographs – some rarely seen before and many unpublished since the 1930s – it will tell of a childhood blighted by family tragedy, and how, as a beautiful young woman, she became the Princess Diana of her day.

It will tell of the love that blossomed with the future King George VI, her beloved Bertie, after they danced together at a lavish May Ball, and how they set about making a family.

It will detail how she instilled confidence in Bertie and helped him overcome his stammer – and how the pair of them were engulfed by the one of the biggest crises ever to face the Royal Family, the abdication of Edward VIII over his forbidden love for Wallis Simpson.

As the new Queen, it was the Queen Mum who picked up the pieces of the shattered Crown afterwards, and set about rebuilding the Royal Family. Since then it has been shaken – sometimes rocked as with the death of Diana in 1997 – but the foundations laid by the Queen Mother at crucial moments in the history of the 20th Century have ensured it has never crumbled.

During the war she was branded 'the most dangerous woman in Europe' by Adolf Hitler ... while rising to new heights of popularity across the world. She insisted that the Royal Family should experience the hardships of the Blitz as the Luftwaffe tried to pound Britain into submission, prompting East Enders to proclaim: 'Ain't she just bloomin' lovely?' Along with the King and Winston Churchill, she became a shining star of an epic drama.

These days she gracefully bears an enduring heartache that began when Bertie died way back in 1952. But she can still count on the love of her daughter The Queen, who calls her simply 'Mummy,' the devotion of grandson Charles – even though she frowns on his relationship with Camilla Parker Bowles – and the warmth of a grateful nation.

As these pages will show, her wit remains as razor-sharp as any comedian and she can still count herself among the world champions of chit-chat. She has even managed to chuckle at THREE premature reports of her death and is not averse to poking fun at herself over her renowned favourite tipple of gin and Dubonnet.

But above all, even though she was a commoner at birth, the Queen Mum still represents the very best of Royalty and the backbone – even though it may be just a little bent now – of the Royal Family. She was married to one monarch, is the mother of the present monarch, grandmother of monarch-in-waiting and great gran of teenage heir Prince William. And as an unswerving traditionalist, she has coached them all on the importance of duty and, well, just being Royal.

When she was 82 the Queen Mum overtook Queen Victoria as the queen who has lived the longest. And just two years ago, on June 14, 1998, she broke another record by usurping Princess Alice as the longest-living member of the Royal Family ever.

Along the way she has gathered ever more admirers – some of them a surprise even to her. Labour MP Willie Hamilton carved a career out of attacking the Monarchy, which he saw as a total waste of time and money. But when the Queen Mum turned 80, even he felt he had to pay tribute.

He said: 'My hatchet is buried, my venom dissipated. I am glad to salute a remarkable old lady. Long may she live to be the pride of her family. And may God understand and forgive me if I have been ensnared and corrupted, if only briefly, by this superb royal trouper.' Even the Queen was moved to salute her mother publicly during her Christmas speech to the nation in 1998. Her Majesty said: 'She has the extraordinary ability to bring happiness to other people's lives. And her own vitality and warmth is returned by those who she meets.' This, then, is the story of the amazing life of an amazing woman. From her birth way back in 1900 to her last remaining ambition – to receive a telegram from her daughter congratulating her on making 100 not out.

1 HER ROYAL WRY-NESS

[left] The Queen Mother holds a charming drawing of a mouse eating some cheese, presented to her outside Clarence House on her 85th birthday.

Throughout her life the Queen Mum has enjoyed a great sense of fun that reflects her love of life. The combination has given her a wry wit dulled not one jot by the passing years – and an ability to deliver a knockout one-liner with all the panache and timing of a stand-up comedian.

Sadly, few have heard her humour or are even aware of it. Whenever she appears on television you can see her lips moving as she talks to well-wishers – or racehorse trainers – but cannot hear her words. Age-old traditions have decreed that silence is golden when it comes to Royal walkabouts, though this is slowly changing as Prince Charles becomes more open.

Newsmen and photographers, though, have witnessed a few memorable Queen Mum moments.

[right] The Queen mother is greeted by well-wishers at Sandringham in July 1990.

And being the nosey parkers they are, they have got to hear of a good few more.

Like the time when she was introduced to travelling to official engagements by helicopter. After a few trips she decided that whirlybirds were wonderful and announced to the pilot: 'The chopper has transformed my life – even more than it transformed Anne Boleyn's.' As she approached her 99th birthday last year, the former Daily Telegraph editor Lord Deedes said: 'In an increasingly earnest world she teaches us all how to have fun – that life should not be all about learning, earning and resting.

'In a world where we have all become workaholics, there she is – about to go into her 100th year – grinning at racehorses. She reminds us that there is life beyond sex, shopping and soccer. Bless her heart.' From time to time, the Queen Mum has even been able to use her wit to defuse politically explosive situations. When she toured South Africa with King George VI in 1947, she came across a bitter Afrikaaner who complained that he could never forgive the English for conquering his country during the Boer War.

Drawing on her Scottish heritage, she flashed her trademark smile and replied at once: 'Oh, I understand that perfectly – we feel very much the same in Scotland.' Newspaper photographers have always considered the Queen Mother a darling – just as Princess Diana was before her shocking death. The Queen Mum knows instinctively how important it is for snappers to get their shots … even if they are sometimes just a tad ill-disciplined, and even if she sometimes has to direct them herself! Just after the Second World War she travelled to the Clyde to inspect a number of Navy vessels, on one of which she had agreed to be

> 'The chopper has transformed my life – even more than it transformed Anne Boleyn's.'

[right] The biggest birthday celebrations to date took place when the Queen Mum reached the age of 99. The crowds which gathered outside her Clarence House home in London were the largest ever and Her Majesty was soon laden down with masses of flowers and brightly-coloured birthday balloons. Driven by her chauffeur Arthur Barty, her golf buggy had become more like a florist's van by the time it had completed its 300 yard journey.

there for two old pence a glass – and Stewart was not slow to take advantage of this generous offer. But his enjoyment was interrupted by the arrival of Her Majesty, who was about to be piped on board.

Gathering up his camera, Stewart rushed upstairs … where the combination of cold air and booze hit him like a bull elephant. Just as the Queen Mum walked by, he collapsed in a heap. The Queen Mother glanced down at him, smiled and turned to an officer to remark: 'I see Mr Stewart hasn't quite found his sea legs.' As she continued her tour, naval ratings dragged Stewart back to the mess, where they poured coffee down his throat so he would be well enough – or at least nearly well enough – to take the picture for which newspapers across the country were leaving huge blank spaces.

Forty minutes later he stumbled back on deck, where the Queen Mum photographed with the ship's company.

A Glasgow snapper named Duncan Stewart, from the now defunct *Bulletin*, was given the job of taking this important picture. As with all official Royal engagements then and now, a rota system operates in which a photographer from one news organisation is allowed to take pictures which are then handed on to all other organisations.

Stewart, who was known to the Queen Mum, dutifully arrived early before the Royal guest and was shown downstairs to the officers' mess. Whisky and gin was being sold

was sitting in a chair with the entire ship's company gathered around her.

Stewart pointed his plate camera at the group and clicked. But the Queen Mother, determined to toy with him, gave him a steady look and said: 'I think you had better take another one, Mr Stewart. Just in case.'

In the days before telephoto lenses and automatic focusing, the Queen Mum was known by photographers as the best judge around of the quaint 'four-yard' rule. This was the distance subjects were required to be from the camera in order to obtain

> 'I see Mr Stewart hasn't quite found his sea legs.'

the best results, a fact of which Her Majesty was keenly aware. While a novice learning his craft, former *Sun* photographer Tony Eyles discovered the secrets of the four-yard rule from the Queen Mum when he was sent to cover a Royal visit to a hospital in Guildford, Surrey.

As she walked down a line of nurses, young Eyles panicked as he tried to adjust the range finder on his camera. A more experienced snapper asked him: 'What's yer problem, young 'un?' and Eyles replied he was having trouble working out distances for his shot. 'Just put it on four yards like the rest of us,' said the older man. 'The Queen Mum is the best judge of four yards in the world.' As Eyles followed the instruction, the Queen Mum picked the prettiest nurse and chatted to her for a while, before both turned to smile at the cameras … exactly four yards away from the snappers, giving them a perfectly sharp picture.

A few years later in 1961, a more experienced Eyles covered another visit, this time to the Tower of London. He was one of ten photographers there to record the event, but a stroppy police inspector insisted on them moving back at least 20 yards from where the Queen Mum's car was due to stop.

A row broke out as the pressmen protested that they would be too far away to get a good shot. One Cockney snapper even told the policeman that the Queen Mum would 'look like a pimple on a pig's arse' in his frame. But the officer doggedly refused to change his mind, so when the Queen Mother arrived the photographers put their cameras on the ground and folded their arms in an impromptu strike.

Unaware of the fracas, the Queen Mum dutifully looked at them so they could shoot away. But while they bowed in respect, there was no snapping. Puzzled, the Queen Mum sent a lady-in-waiting over to the photographers. She was told why no pictures were being taken, though the reference to the 'pig's arse' was NOT repeated.

The lady-in-waiting scuttled back to the Queen Mum and explained. Within seconds, a quiet word was whispered in the inspector's ear and the snappers were allowed to move back to their original position. The Queen Mum returned to her car, turned, smiled and said: 'Good morning, gentlemen. Are we having a nice day?' Eyles went on to spend the best part of 40 years photographing the Royal Family. And he says of the Queen Mum: 'She is the only one for whom I would have laid my coat over a puddle like Sir Walter Raleigh.' Another snapper who followed the Royals for years is gritty Scot Ken Lennox, now Picture Editor of the *News of the World*. For many years he worked for the *Daily Express*, based in Aberdeen, and spent more hours than he cares to remember photographing various members of the Royal Family

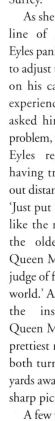

[above] The Queen mother strolls near her fishing lodge on the banks of the River Dee on the royal estate of Balmoral. The lodge was a birthday present from other members of the family to celebrate her 80th birthday. She entertains there winter and summer and even in her mid 80s was still pulling salmon from the river.

[above left] The Queen Mother celebrating her 89th birthday at Clarence House still manages a wave and a smile despite being laden down with flowers and home-made birthday cards.

[overleaf] In 1982 the Queen Mother and her houseguests were visiting the famous beach at Holcombe in Norfolk, where many years later Gwyneth Paltrow filmed the last scene for her Oscar-winning film *Shakespeare in Love*. The only one of her guests to go swimming that day was the Duke of Grafton. After his swim he couldn't find his clothes as he had got changed in the sand dunes. A major search was launched under the Queen Mother's direction, with the police and the rest of the party combing the beach to find the peer's missing outfit.

as they headed to and from the Balmoral estate.

One day in 1970, he climbed out of bed early as the Queen Mother was due to fly out of Balmoral by helicopter en route for an aircraft carrier in the North Sea. It was a misty morning and Lennox hung around waiting for the chopper to take off, but there was no sign of any action. Eventually a Jaguar pulled up nearby, an official climbed out and told Lennox the Royal Flight from Balmoral had been cancelled. However, he added that it would take off from Aberdeen's Dyce airport 50 miles away.

Lennox asked: 'Where is the Queen Mother now?' The official replied: 'She's in the back of the car. She says that if you leave now, we'll drive slowly and you will get your photo in Aberdeen.' A disbelieving

Lennox glanced round to see the Queen Mum sitting in the back of the Jag, giving him a little wave.

He jumped in his car and headed for Aberdeen. At Dyce airport, the Queen Mum turned as she boarded the helicopter and waved regally as though she was being seen off by a crowd of thousands. In fact, only Lennox and the airport manager were there.

Lennox had another reason to be grateful to the Queen Mum during a visit to the Royal Ballet. He was due to be the official 'rota' photographer for the book-signing ceremony – a dull assignment as book-signing normally produces somewhat bland pictures. But on his arrival he saw a pretty young ballerina practising a spectacular routine.

The wily photographer learned that the girl had

been chosen to present a bouquet to the Queen Mum. She was due to dance in front of the Royal visitor before plunging into the deepest of curtsies, at the same time gracefully stretching up her hand to present the flowers.

Lennox reckoned he could quickly snap the book signing then rush outside to get what he was sure would be a much more interesting shot of the ballerina's perfect presentation, which, he knew, 'would sail into the paper.' But he reckoned without a strict Royal detective, who insisted no one should move inside the room used for the book signing.

The Queen Mother came in and – as she put pen to paper – used the old trick of asking the date so that

Lennox could prepare to take his picture.

Click! Lennox had his shot and turned to rush for the exit. But suddenly the detective grabbed him, pushed him up against a wall and barked: 'Wait!' It was clear that no amount of pleading from the desperate Lennox would persuade him to release his iron grip. Then the Queen Mum strolled past. And seeing Ken pinned against the wall, she looked at him and said: 'Shouldn't you be outside for this picture?' With that, the detective's arm miraculously melted away and Ken took up his position for what turned out to be a 'great snap.'

My colleague Arthur Edwards, *The Sun*'s renowned Royal snapper, was sent to cover the Queen Mum's

[below left] The one that got away from Arthur. The gondolier had followed Arthur's instructions to the letter and handed a Cornetto to the Queen Mum. Unfortunately it was on the wrong side of the canal which gave Ron Bell the picture and not Arthur. The Cornetto featured in one of the most popular TV advertisements of the day and, needless to say, next day the picture appeared everywhere.

official visit to Venice in 1984 ... and grimly remembers 'the one that got away.' Arthur knew that like all visitors to Venice, the Queen Mother would be taken for a trip on a gondola. One of the most popular TV adverts of the day was for Cornetto ice cream, featuring a gondolier singing *Just One Cornetto* opera-style. So Arthur cheekily persuaded the Queen Mum's gondolier to give her a Cornetto.

She readily accepted and Arthur excitedly waited for the gondola to get in the right position. But to his dismay, at the last minute it berthed on the far side of the canal – and all Arthur could see was Her Majesty's back.

'I called for her to turn round,' said Arthur. 'But the Rear Admiral of the Royal Yacht *Britannia*, Sir Paul Greening, snatched the Cornetto from her. When she turned and waved she was empty-handed.' Arthur then caught a glimpse of Ron Bell, a pal but a rival snapper who worked for the Press Association. He was grinning from ear to ear as he had been standing near the spot where the gondola berthed – and had got the Cornetto shot. Every paper used Bell's picture the next day but at least he thanked Arthur for dreaming up the stunt.

Many of the Queen Mum's finest gags have been at the expense of her daughter – or herself.

Once, as mother and daughter had lunch together in the library of Clarence House, the Queen Mum's

[below] When the Queen Mother made a visit to Venice in support of the British 'Venice in Peril' Fund, the trip meant she fulfilled a lifelong ambition to see the city. Usually taking a trip in a Gondola means a romantic ride, but her companion on this occasion was the then captain of the Royal Yacht *Britannia*, Rear Admiral Sir Paul Greening.

[left and below left] The Queen Mother has frequently met members of the same family – but years apart. A good example of this happened to two members of Arthur Edwards's immediate family. Her Majesty first met his grandmother Alice Ward in 1960 and then 20 years later met his daughter Annmarie at a flower show. Alice, aged 80, was a member of the St Katherine's Settlement Day Centre where pensioners met to socialise with a cup of tea and a friendly game of cards. The Queen Mother, the centre's patron, dropped in and found Alice and her friend Lil Golding playing cards. The Queen Mother asked what game they were playing, but they explained they were having fun telling their fortunes through the cards. Annmarie's meeting came when she went with her dad on a job to photograph the Queen Mother at the Sandringham Flower Show just before her 80th birthday. Unknown to her dad, she had made the Queen Mother a birthday card. While Arthur photographed the Queen Mother touring the trade stands, out popped Annemarie to present the card. The most surprised person was Arthur when he saw his own daughter through his viewfinder in the frame with the Queen Mum. But the surprise was not over for Annmarie: a few weeks later a letter arrived from Clarence House with a thank-you note from the Queen Mother – a treasured memento which she has kept until this day.

[above right] Each year the Queen Mother visits retired Sandringham estate workers. In 1978 she took Princess Margaret with her to visit Ted Grist and his wife.

[right] There is nothing like a good gossip and chat over the garden fence. Here the Queen Mum enjoys an exchange of news with 90 year-old Ted Smith, another retired worker at Anmer near Sandringham in 1980.

official residence, the Queen asked her: 'Might I have another glass of wine?' The Queen Mum put on a serious expression and replied: 'Is that wise? You know you have to reign all afternoon.' A few years ago as the Royals enjoyed a family holiday at Balmoral, the Queen suggested a picnic in one of the vast estate's remote lodges. The idea, though attractive, involved a great deal of effort. Land Rovers had to be packed and driven in driving rain along muddy, pot-holed tracks. But the effort was made.

Eventually the Royal convoy arrived at the lodge and everyone scrambled out to head for the door, only to find it locked. The Queen, Prince Philip and other members of the family glanced at each other with accusing looks meaning: 'Who's got the key?' They knew it would take hours for a courtier to drive back to the main house for the key, and for a moment it seemed certain that a massive family argument would erupt.

Just then the Queen Mum arrived – and the Queen marched over to explain the predicament. The Queen Mum consoled her daughter, and looking over her shoulder at the rest of the family said: 'Oh my poor

> 'Oh my poor darling. But I thought you were the Queen and all you had to say was "Open Sesame".'

darling. But I thought you were the Queen and all you had to say was "Open Sesame".' Everyone burst out laughing.

A stonking row did explode once among staff at Clarence House, which held up service of a meal to the Queen Mother. A number of gays are employed in the household and the Queen Mum dispatched a flunkey to the kitchen with the words: 'My compliments to the old queens down there, but this old queen is hungry and wants her dinner.'

Her Majesty's love of fine wines is legendary and her daily tipple of a gin and Dubonnet certainly seems to have kept her active. On one occasion she visited a notable garden whose owner was warned in advance that she would stay to tea … and possibly linger afterwards for a drink.

The Queen Mum did stay on and without thinking, her lady host blurted out: 'I hear you like gin.' As she realised what she had said, the woman hoped a hole would open up beneath her so she could disappear. But without batting an eyelid, the Queen Mother replied: 'I hadn't realised I enjoyed that reputation. But as I do, perhaps you could make it a large one.'

[right] July 16, 1987. Ever since the days of the Blitz the Queen Mother has held a special place in her heart for London's East End – and they for her. She went on a 'pub crawl' as part of a tour of gardens and stopped at the Queen's Head in Stepney. The landlord offered her a glass of champagne. With a smile on her face she said: 'No thank you. Might I have a pint of bitter please?' She happily knocked back a pint and said it was like 'being in *EastEnders*.' She said she had seen the TV soap occasionally, but added: 'It's nice to see the real thing. Champagne is wonderful, but I think I will make bitter my drink in future.'

[left] The Queen Mum waves to the crowds on her 99th birthday, flanked by her great grandsons Prince Harry aged 15 and Prince William, 17 and also accompanied by Prince Charles.

2 LOVELY EYES AND GERMAN SPIES

[left] Even from an early age the captivating eyes of Elizabeth Bowes Lyon were one of her strongest features. Never in her wildest dreams would this young girl have believed she would become Britain's best-loved lady of the century.

[right] The head of the family, the Earl of Strathmore

[below] A Glamis family group taken in 1902, the year that Elizabeth's brother David was born. In all Lord and Lady Strathmore had 10 children but the eldest Violet, born in 1882, had died of diphtheria in 1893.

Queen Victoria was still on the throne and Britain was engaged in its last Imperial war against the Boers in South Africa. The Wright Brothers had yet to launch their new-fangled invention, the aeroplane. Horses were still the preferred mode of transport over the motor car and the average weekly wage was less than £2. It was into this long-lost world on August 4 1900 that Elizabeth Angela Marguerite Bowes Lyon, the future Queen and Queen Mother, was born.

She was the ninth child of the Earl and Countess of Strathmore – and although not Royal, her pedigree was formidable. On her father's side she could trace her ancestors back to Robert the Bruce and other Scottish warlords, and her mother was descended from the Duke of Portland, Prime Minister to the 'mad' King, George III.

The Strathmores were a well-established landowning family, extremely wealthy and well-connected to high society. The family seat was Glamis Castle in Angus – the fabled home of Shakespeare's Macbeth. But there were other homes in St James's Square, London, the rambling estate of St Paul's Walden Bury near Hitchin, Herts, and Streatlam Castle amid the coalfields of County Durham.

Elizabeth's father, whom she adored, was late registering her birth and was fined 7s 6d (37p) for his misdemeanour. His tardiness triggered a mystery that has never been solved over the Queen Mum's birthplace. It is clearly stated as Hitchin on her birth certificate, but she has insisted that she was born in London. One theory is that she is indeed a true Londoner but that her father, realising he was late with the registration and being in Hitchin at the time she was born, told a porkie and registered her there to save his travelling to the capital.

At the time of Elizabeth's birth her eldest sibling May was already 17. Following May came Patrick, Jock, Alexander, Fergus, Rose and Michael. Elizabeth

The Queen Mum **HER FIRST 100 YEARS**

would have had another big sister, Violet, but she died of heart problems brought on by diphtheria in 1893 when she was 11. Twenty-one months after Elizabeth was born, the Strathmores had a tenth child, David. The two youngest tots soon teamed up and their mother christened them 'My little Benjamins.' The pair formed a close bond and were known as mischievous but full of charm. At Glamis Castle, they would climb the stone steps to the ramparts and throw buckets of water over the side to repel imaginary invaders. And even then, Elizabeth displayed an infectious love of

> On one occasion she bluntly announced 'I like people' to one of the many groups of guests entertained by the family.

life. On one occasion she bluntly announced 'I like people' to one of the many groups of guests entertained by the family. It was a trait she would retain throughout her 100 years.

Amazingly, Elizabeth first rubbed shoulders with her future husband Prince Albert, second son of the then Prince of Wales, at a children's party when she was just FOUR and he was nine. She thought the shy lad looked sad – and offered him the cherries from the top of her chocolate cake. The pair saw each other again a few years later on June 22 1911. Elizabeth and her sisters were outside

[above left] 1904: Elizabeth aged four with her beloved brother David, aged three. They were inseparable and were nicknamed 'my two Benjamins' by their mother, Lady Strathmore because of the number of pranks they carried out. 1904 was also the year that their father Lord Glamis succeeded to the Earldom of Strathmore.

[above] David and Elizabeth playing together, with the gardens of St Paul's in the background. In later life David lived at St Paul's Walden Bury – the family home – and served as Lord Lieutenant of Hertfordshire. He was appointed a Knight Commander of the Royal Victorian Order and died in 1961.

[above right] To their disgust, David and Elizabeth were made to dress up by their mother and to perform for the benefit of the grown-ups. David wears a jester's costume and Elizabeth a pink and silver dress copied from a painting by Velázquez.

Westminster Abbey watching the procession taking Albert's father to his coronation as King George V.

It was a big year for Elizabeth, for she also went away on her first foreign holiday with little brother David. The excited youngsters were taken for a tour of the beautiful Italian city of Florence. But joy turn to terrible sadness on their return. Their brother Alexander died of an illness which has never been explained. The following year, the little Benjamins were separated as David was sent to a boarding school in Broadstairs, Kent, in preparation for studies at Eton. Life went on for Elizabeth. But for her and everyone else, it was soon to change dramatically as Britain went to war with Germany.

By a quirk of fate, the simmering conflict came to a head on Elizabeth's 14th birthday – August 4 1914.

The teenager woke up to celebrate the date in the Strathmores' St James's Square home, having breakfast in bed and opening telegrams of congratulation and a pile of presents wrapped in brightly-coloured paper. There was also a birthday reward from her parents for passing her Oxford Local exam with distinction. It was a box that night at London's Coliseum Theatre, where her favourite actor Charles Hawtrey – later to find fame as a wimpish twit in the *Carry On* films – was performing. Also on the bill were Lipinsky's Dog Comedians, jugglers Moran & Wise and the Russian ballerina Fedorovna.

Excited Elizabeth had one of the most magical times of her life at the show, laughing, cheering and applauding wildly. But as the curtain fell troops were already beginning to assemble in their barracks.

[left] Elizabeth aged seven photographed for an official portrait on her birthday.

[below right] Elizabeth at Glamis Castle with a pull-along toy horse. Horses were to become her lifelong passion.

[below] Even as a toddler, Elizabeth knew how to pose for a photographer. She was to enchant photographers in the years ahead when she became first Duchess of York and later Queen.

Mobilisation had begun. Later that evening Elizabeth's future father-in-law George V wrote in his diary: 'I held a Council at 10.45 to declare war with Germany. It is a terrible catastrophe, but it is not our fault. An enormous crowd collected outside the Palace; we went on the balcony both before and after dinner.' Across the land, eager young men rushed to join up to fight for King and country. Three of Elizabeth's brothers, Patrick, Jock and Fergus – who were serving with the Black Watch – hurried to rejoin their regiment. And a fourth brother, Michael, abandoned his studies at Oxford's Magdalen College to enlist in the Royal Scots. The rest of the family, including Elizabeth, moved north to Glamis.

History and legend echoed around the castle's 15ft thick red sandstone walls. Shakespeare based King Duncan's murder by Macbeth there and its previous occupants included Mary, Queen of Scots, Bonnie Prince Charlie and the Duke of Cumberland – 'the butcher of Culloden'. Now, Lady Strathmore decided to write one more chapter in its annals. Determined to help the war effort, she turned Glamis's grand banqueting hall into a convalescent home for soldiers wounded at the front. Two rows of eight iron beds were lined up against its oak-panelled walls and by Christmas the first unlucky victims of the trenches were arriving.

The young Elizabeth helped to look after them, showing a natural gift for caring uncannily similar to another blue-blooded girl who married into the Royal Family decades later – Princess Diana, the Queen of Hearts. There were no cameras or reporters around to record Elizabeth's acts of kindness. But as she walked from bed to bed, chatting to the bloodied soldiers in

a white blouse and long black skirt, they came to adore her.

She knew them all by their Christian names and wrote letters to loved-ones for those who were unable to use their hands. She played cards and dominoes with them and ran errands to buy their packets of Navy Cut or Gold Flake tobacco. She took the walking wounded for walks in the grounds as they convalesced. Elizabeth remembered every soldier's birthday, made sure they had gifts to lift their spirits and sang Happy Birthday to them as her mother played the piano. In a warm tribute, one appreciative soldier wrote of her: 'She had the loveliest eyes, expressive and eloquent eyes, and a very taking way of knitting her forehead when speaking. For all her fifteen years she was very womanly, kind-hearted and sympathetic.' There were other duties for the teenager to perform. When she wasn't nursing, she joined the other women of Glamis in knitting

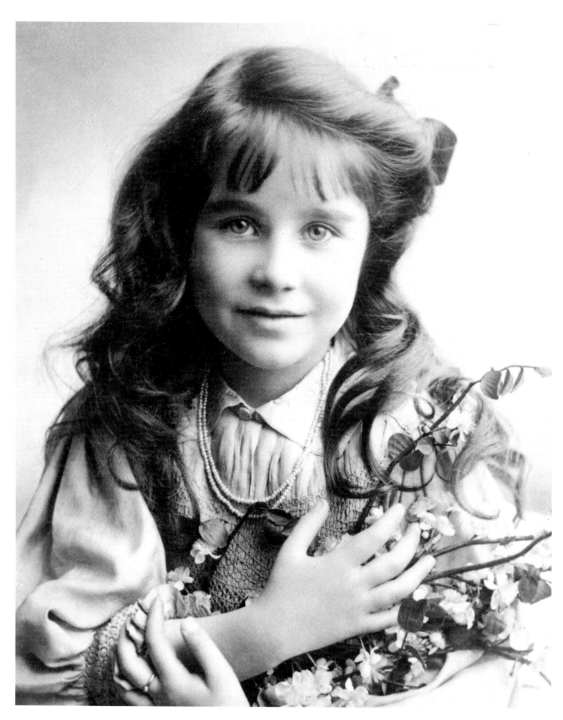

scarves, mittens and socks. And as the number of patients at the castle increased, she also had to stuff hand-made sleeping bags with tissue paper – used instead of down for insulation. Years later she recalled: 'My chief occupation was crumpling the paper until it was so soft it wouldn't crackle when put into the linings.' Despite the uplifting atmosphere at Glamis, these were dark days indeed. In April 1915 London was bombed by a German zeppelin. A month later a German submarine sank the passenger ship *Lusitania*, killing more than 1,000 passengers and crew. And

tragedy struck the Strathmores in September when Elizabeth's brother Fergus lost his life at the Battle of Loos. In a grim scene that was repeated in countless homes up and down the country, a messenger boy arrived at Glamis and handed a telegram to Elizabeth's sister Rose. The distraught Rose showed it to Elizabeth, who ran with it to her mother.

Fergus died in the battle on September 25, one of 48,267 British casualties. He was 26 and had just celebrated his first wedding anniversary while on leave at Glamis before returning to the front. The tears

[above] Elizabeth aged seven, again posing for the cameras as she cradles an armful of wild flowers. This picture, which shows her early love of pearls, is regarded as a family favourite.

[right] In the latter stages of the Great War Elizabeth shows how she has grown into the beautiful young woman whose hand was to be won by the stammering Bertie.

flowed at the castle over his death. Lady Strathmore was so inconsolable that she had to leave the running of Glamis to her daughters.

Tragedy almost struck again the following year when the central keep of the castle caught fire, though fortunately most of the recovering patients were away from their beds at the cinema. Elizabeth rang the fire brigade but then she and brother David organised everyone into a human chain to pass buckets of water towards the flames. Her actions undoubtedly saved the castle, with all its valuable paintings and furniture, from burning down. The local paper, the *Dundee Courier*, recorded the drama by hailing her as 'a veritable heroine' for the salvage work she performed even within the fire zone. In 1917 the dreaded telegram boy called again with the news that another brother, Michael, was missing in action, presumed dead. But this time, after an agonising three months delay, word reached Glamis that in fact he had been wounded and was a prisoner of war.

But it wasn't until 1998, in a BBC documentary, that Elizabeth's most amazing act of the First World War was revealed … the nailing of a German spy. It happened during the winter of 1917, when she took a break from Glamis to visit her sister Rose, then 27. Rose was living temporarily at Felixstowe, Suffolk,

while her Navy officer husband, who went on to become a vice-admiral, was at war. Her semi-detached house had paper-thin walls backing on to a dentist's surgery. And the dentist, it seemed, was in the habit of plying soldiers and sailors with drink after treating them late into the evening.

As their suspicions grew, Elizabeth and Rose crept outside one night and hid behind bushes by the surgery. They heard sailors telling the dentist where they were going and what they were going to do. And to them, it was clear the dentist was not just extracting

[below left] An informal portrait of Elizabeth seated in an armchair.

[below left and right] From the mischievous 'young Benjamin', Elizabeth grew into one of the most attractive young debutantes of her generation, a beauty which soon attracted the attention of the Duke of York.

[below left] An informal portrait of Elizabeth seated in an armchair.

teeth, but using booze to extract military secrets that he would then give the Germans. Rose's daughter, Lady Mary Clayton, told the documentary how the sisters passed on the information to the admiral in charge of the area, Lord Fisher of Kilverstone, and in due course were thrilled to see police marching up to the house next door and taking the dentist away. He was later released so he could feed bogus 'secrets' to the Germans. King George got to hear of the sisters' whistle-blowing and was all for giving them medals, but they modestly played down the incident and said:

[above right] Elizabeth surveys the scene from an upper window at the family home at Glamis.

[above] Despite the apparent ease of her upbringing, Elizabeth experienced personally the sorrows of the First World, as she lost her brother Fergus and for three months believed her brother Michael had died.

The Queen Mum **HER FIRST 100 YEARS**

[left] Elizabeth, with her mother Lady Strathmore. Elizabeth was the second youngest of Lady Strathmore's ten children.

[below left] After the war, Elizabeth poses with her devoted brother David, in a picture from the Bowes Lyon family album. The war had forced her to grow up quickly and the tragedy had hit her personally with the loss of her older brother Fergus.

[right] Another photograph from the family album. Her warmth, humour and cheerfulness made her popular with the wounded soldiers who were convalescing at Glamis Castle. One soldier, who went back to the front after being cared for by the young Elizabeth, tied a label to his tunic which read: 'Please return to Glamis' in case he was injured again.

[left] January 1923: Elizabeth at the family home at Bruton Street in Mayfair at the time of her engagement to Bertie.

'Oh no, don't do that.' During the war the King's youngest son, by now known as Bertie, was trying to establish himself as a naval officer. He was desperate to serve his country but the ill-health that plagued his childhood was still causing him problems. He was rushed ashore from his ship *HMS Collingwood* to have his appendix removed, then suffered acute stomach pains which resulted in him being given a desk job at the Admiralty. Bertie became bored, unhappy and restless. But in May 1916 he was returned to Collingwood – and at last he found himself covered in glory at the Battle of Jutland.

When the order 'for action' was given, Bertie rushed to his position at Turret A and stayed firmly there until the battle was over. He was commended in dispatches by Admiral Sir John Jellicoe and promoted to full lieutenant. It was a timely morale-booster for Bertie. Until then he had been living in utter fear – of his father, a strict disciplinarian who once said: 'My father was frightened of his father, I was frightened of my father and I am damn well going to see to it that my children are frightened of me!' In a letter Bertie wrote to his brother the Prince of Wales, later Edward VIII, he said: 'When I was on top of the turret I never felt any fear of shells or anything else. It seems curious but all sense of danger and everything else goes except the one longing to deal death in every possible way to the enemy.' In 1918 the war, which cost ten million lives, mercifully ground to a halt. But it was another year before the last patient left Glamis Castle. By now the maturing Elizabeth was emerging as one of the prettiest debutantes of her generation, and was presented at Court in Edinburgh's Holyroodhouse Palace during the King and Queen's summer stay there. After the rigours of the war, her life became a breezier round of parties and social events such as the races at Ascot and Henley regatta. At balls, her dance card was always full. But one young man in particular caught her eye.

Jamie Stuart was the dashing third son of the Earl of Moray. He had been to Eton with Elizabeth's brother Michael and served with him in the Royal Scots, earning the Military Cross for heroism during the Battle of the Somme. He was also a wonderful dancer – and the newly-appointed equerry to Prince Albert. On May 20 1920 Elizabeth was invited to a May Ball thrown by Lord and Lady Farquhar at their home in London's Grosvenor Square. Jamie Stuart was there … and so was Bertie.

3 HAVING A BALL WITH BERTIE

Bertie stood at the side of the ballroom as he watched his equerry Jamie Stuart do the foxtrot with the girl who he was sure was the most beautiful on the floor, Elizabeth Bowes Lyon. But there was one problem. Jamie and Elizabeth were close friends and many in their circle were already wondering if they would marry, especially as Jamie had broken off an engagement to the daughter of a prosperous Glasgow trader. Bertie knew Elizabeth in as much as he remembered their occasional meetings as children. But all he cared about now was taking a turn on the dancefloor with her. When he made his intentions clear to Jamie, the equerry gallantly and politely withdrew. Bertie asked Elizabeth to dance and she graciously accepted. By the end of the evening Cupid's arrow was firmly embedded in the King's second son, and soon afterwards Jamie found himself relieved of his Royal post and despatched to the faraway oilfields of Oklahoma! It was hardly love at first sight for Elizabeth, however, particularly as Bertie still spoke with a stammer he had suffered from childhood. And it wasn't as if she had any shortage of suitors. As diarist Chips Channon recorded, she was regarded as mildly flirtatious in an old-fashioned sort of way. He added: 'She makes every man feel chivalrous and gallant towards her.' Undaunted, and even though he was living in the shadow of his more glamorous brother David, Prince of Wales, Bertie continued his pursuit. He even blurted out to his mother, Queen Mary, that he had found his ideal love. He told her she must see for herself – and she did just that, driving to visit the Strathmores at Glamis. Mary was deeply impressed with the way Elizabeth deputised as host for her sick mother and immediately thought she would make an ideal bride. Not for Bertie, though, but for the Prince of Wales. However, apart from discussing the prospect with her closest friends, she did nothing. Bertie, now with the title Duke of York, perked up when he was

invited to Glamis by the Strathmores. They did not see him as a possible suitor but he was determined to win the heart of the girl from the May Ball. He sent out all the right signals but although Elizabeth was friendly, she kept him at arm's length. Bertie tried two proposals of marriage but was rejected each time. His prospects were hardly enhanced when his father tactlessly told him: 'You'll be a lucky fellow if she'll

have you.' Over the New Year in 1923 Bertie, sensing that Elizabeth might be warming to him, steeled himself to make a third proposal. But on January 5 he got the shock of his life – along with the rest of the country – when the *Daily News* published a bombshell story under the headlines:

SCOTTISH BRIDE FOR PRINCE OF WALES
Heir to the Throne to Wed Peer's Daughter
An Official Announcement Imminent

Elizabeth was not named in the story but it was clear it referred to her. She was just as stunned as Bertie – not to mention the playboy Prince of Wales, who took the rare step of issuing a denial. A Royal household statement said: 'A few days ago the Daily News announced the forthcoming engagement of the Prince of Wales to an Italian Princess. Today the same journal states on what is claimed to be unquestionable authority that the formal announcement of His Royal Highness's engagement to a daughter of a Scottish peer will be made within the next few months. We are officially authorised to say that this report is as devoid of foundation as was the previous.' A few days later Bertie was invited to spend the weekend at the Strathmores' Hertfordshire home. As he walked with

Elizabeth in the garden he plucked up the courage to ask for her hand once again. To his delight, this time she said Yes. He immediately sent a telegram to the King, who was staying at Sandringham, with the simple message: 'All right. Bertie.' Then he followed the telegram to the Norfolk estate to ask his father formally for permission to marry Elizabeth. An official announcement followed swiftly. It read: 'It is with the greatest of pleasure that the King and Queen announce the betrothal of their beloved son, the Duke of York, to the Lady Elizabeth Bowes Lyon, daughter of the Earl and Countess of Strathmore, to which union the King has gladly given his consent.' Elizabeth set about preparing for her future life as Duchess of York and daughter-in-law of King George V. Winning over the King was no easy task, for she knew he ruled his own children with an iron fist. But she refused to be intimidated by him and quickly garnered his affection with her charm. He was an obsessive stickler for punctuality but became so enamoured with her that he even let her get away with being late for dinner one night. Instead of bawling at her as she entered the dining room, he said: 'You are not late, my dear. I think we must have sat down two minutes early.' Elizabeth did fall foul of him once, though, when she broke a golden Royal rule by

[above] Elizabeth and Bertie at their wedding in Westminster Abbey in 1923. She has kept her wedding dress in a wardrobe at Clarence House to this day.

[above] The newly-weds appear on the balcony at Buckingham palace.

giving a brief interview to a newspaper. An enterprising reporter from the *Daily Sketch*, the most popular tabloid of its day, caught up with her when it was announced she had a sapphire engagement ring. With a captivating smile, Elizabeth told him: 'It is all very embarrassing. I've never been in such demand before and it takes a little while to get used to it. I shan't see the Duke of York all day because he's out hunting. But I expect he will slip around for a little while later this evening – I hope so at any rate. You ask me about my plans but I can't, you see, because there aren't any yet.' The harmless interview was nothing compared to the startling 'three people in our marriage' revelations of Princess Diana on TV's *Panorama* programme, or Prince Charles's confession of his affair with Camilla Parker Bowles during his telly talk with Jonathan Dimbleby. But the King, thinking it outrageous that Elizabeth should allow the masses a glimpse of her private life, flew into a rage. And an equerry was duly dispatched to give her a stern telling-off. From that

> 'Elizabeth is with us now,' she said. 'So well brought up, a great addition to the family.'

day, the Queen Mum has NEVER given another interview. And she was utterly appalled when Charles and Di went public with their damaging disclosures. Despite the minor hiccup, Bertie's mother wrote glowingly of her future daughter-in-law. 'Elizabeth is with us now,' she said. 'So well brought up, a great addition to the family.' King George decreed that the wedding should be a grand public spectacle to brighten the post-war Depression. Bertie wore the uniform of a Group Captain of the Royal Air Force and his bride wore a dress of ivory chiffon with a train of Point de Flandres lace, which she keeps to this day in a wardrobe at Clarence House. Queen Mary gave Elizabeth a diamond and sapphire necklace as a wedding gift, while the King offered a tiara. From her father Elizabeth received a diamond tiara and a necklace of pearls and diamonds. Bertie gave her another diamond and pearl necklace and she gave him a dress watch chain of platinum and pearls. The newly-formed British Broadcasting Corporation asked if they

42

[left] Throughout her long Royal
career, the Queen Mother always
been the recipient of flowers
from young admirers. Here she
receives a bouquet at the
Richmond Royal Horse Show in
July 1923.

[right] The Duke and Duchess of
York visit the Cheyne Hospital for
Children in July 1923.

[right] Elizabeth arrives at Ascot
in 1924. Three-quarters of a
century later the Ascot races
were still to be an annual fixture
in the Queen Mum's calendar.

London by train to honeymoon first at the home of a mutual friend in Polesden Lacey, Surrey, and then at Glamis. But unfortunately the Scottish weather was so bad that the new Duchess went down with whooping cough, which she later described as 'not a very romantic disease.' On their return to London the couple headed for their new home, White Lodge in Richmond Park — originally built as a hunting lodge by George II. Elizabeth set about her Royal duties with vigour and she and Bertie soon had a long list of official engagements to fulfil. The Royal newcomer also used her confidence to boost her husband's.

[left] The Duchess of York sits elegantly for a formal photograph, eight months after the birth of her first child and just before she and her husband set out for a visit to Australia and New Zealand in early 1927.

could broadcast the ceremony on the wireless. But the idea was vetoed by the Archbishop of Canterbury because 'the service might be received by persons in public houses with their hats on.' Elizabeth travelled to Westminster Abbey in a state landau with Lord Strathmore at her side, becoming the first Royal bride married at the Abbey since Princess Anne of Bohemia wed Richard II. Three thousand guests were invited including 30 factory boys to mark Bertie's enthusiasm for the youth movement. Guests noted that as Elizabeth entered the Abbey, she placed her wedding bouquet on the tomb of the unknown soldier. It was not part of the schedule and is believed to have been a remembrance gesture for her fallen brother Fergus. As she took her oaths she became Her Royal Highness The Duchess of York, with the status of Princess. Bertie had a shorter and somewhat less formal pet name for her. He called her 'Ducks.' After celebrations at Buckingham Palace the couple left

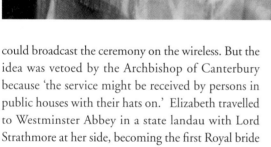

Bertie had a shorter and somewhat less formal pet name for her. He called her 'Ducks.'

She persuaded him to see a speech therapist, an Australian named Lionel Logue, who taught him how to alter his breathing to suppress his stammer. Bertie's self-assurance was further enhanced by the very fact that Elizabeth was at his side. When he had to make a speech she sat mouthing the words, occasionally touching his hand for comfort. The speech lessons worked so well that Bertie wrote a thank-you note to Mr Logue, proudly telling him that even his father could now understand him. All was not sweetness and light, however. Bertie, a skilled tennis player who took part in the 1926 men's doubles tournament at Wimbledon, was a chain smoker prone to flashes of ill-temper. Occasionally it was aggravated by Elizabeth's lack of punctuality and he would often be found restlessly pacing corridors as he waited for her. But she was able to take it in her stride and even managed to force him to smile by mockingly taking his pulse and counting: 'Tick, tick, tick. One, two, [far right] The Duke and Duchess of York accompanied by local dignitaries during a visit to Eastbourne.

[right] The Queen Mother was heard to remark during the Second World War that she did not care to wear uniform as she had only donned one in her life, that of a Guide leader, and it did not suit her. Here, in 1927, she is seen in that uniform, in the company of the Duke of York.

[below] The Duchess of York takes a quiet moment off from the royal round of inspections, hospital visits and overseas trips.

[above right] The Duke and Duchess of York visit Loughton in Essex, shortly after their marriage in 1923.

[right] December 1927: the Duchess of York inspects the King's Own Yorkshire Light Regiment, of which she was the Colonel-in-Chief.

three.' On April 21 1926, the Yorks started a family as their first child, Elizabeth Alexandra Mary, was born, and made a new beginning at a permanent home in London's Piccadilly. Incredibly, considering the fuss it would cause today, the birth was of only moderate interest to the nation's newspapers. They were far more concerned with industrial unrest and the prospect of a General Strike. Miners in particular were in militant mood following a threat from pit owners to cut their wages. When the Yorks' baby, dubbed Lilibet, was just eight months old, the couple were asked by the King to undertake a six-month tour of Australia and New Zealand. Unlike today, there were no jets available and they travelled Down Under on the battleship *Renown*. It was a tough assignment but the Duchess turned it into a roaring success despite falling ill with tonsillitis in the early stages.

[far left] In October 1923 the Yorks visited Serbia for the christening of the Serbian Crown Prince and the wedding of Prince Paul of Serbia to Princess Olga of Greece. Here they leave from Victoria Station at the start of their trip.

[left] The Duke and Duchess of York at the opening of York House in November 1926. The 18th-century house in Twickenham had been acquired in 1923 by the civic authority for its municipal offices.

[below] The Duke and Duchess of York on their visit to Australia in 1927. They were received by a crowd of over 50,000 when they attended the state opening of parliament in Canberra.

47

[above] These strikingly similar poses over sixty years apart of Diana Princess of Wales and the Queen Mother echo the air of modernity which they both seemed to bring to their respective roles in the early years of their marriages.

[right] The Duchess of York photographed with friends on Whitehall in 1925

THIS STONE
WAS LAID BY
H.R.H.
THE DUCHESS OF YORK
ON
NOVEMBER 29TH 1928

She set about inventing the Royal walkabout, now an integral part of Royal life, by making eye contact with one or two onlookers rather than just offering a catch-all glance at the crowd. It turned out to be a brilliant strategy. The Aussies loved her just as all crowds have throughout her life. Bertie had to make THREE speeches one morning. But by now he had perfect confidence in himself and did not hesitate at all. The couple were met with an increasing round of public duties upon their return. Bertie became heavily [right] The Duchess of York with the future Queen Elizabeth II as a baby, in May 1926. The child's full name was Elizabeth Alexandra Mary, but her parents dubbed her 'Lilibet'.

[left] The Duchess of York laying the foundation stone of a new wing at the London Fever Hospital in November 1928. From soon after her marriage, Elizabeth took on an ever-increasing round of royal engagements, both domestic and overseas.

involved in organisations ranging from the Industrial Welfare Society to Dr Barnardo's, while the Duchess concentrated on hospitals and child welfare. After one ceremony, a newspaper observed: 'She lays a foundation stone as if she has just discovered a new and delightful way of spending an afternoon.' Whenever possible, the couple liked to carry out engagements together, and there was not the slightest hint of any Charles and Diana-type rivalry between the two. On August 21 1930, their second daughter Margaret Rose was born at Glamis Castle in the middle of a thunderstorm, becoming the first Royal baby born north of the border since 1602. And soon afterwards the family moved into Royal Lodge, Windsor, which the Queen Mum still counts as a home. They were close-knit and seemed to have little in common with the Prince of Wales, whose name was linked in the gossip columns to a string of married women. In November 1930, he travelled to Melton Mowbray in Leicestershire to meet friends. Among the others there was a 34-year-old American woman named Wallis Simpson and her husband Ernest. Fate was about to take a hand and dramatically change the lives of the Duke and Duchess of York forever.

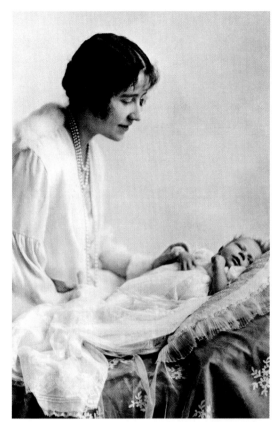

[right] The Duchess of York with her second daughter, Princess Margaret. The baby was born at Glamis, meaning the Home Secretary, who by ancient tradition had to be present at each royal birth, was forced to make the long trip to Scotland.

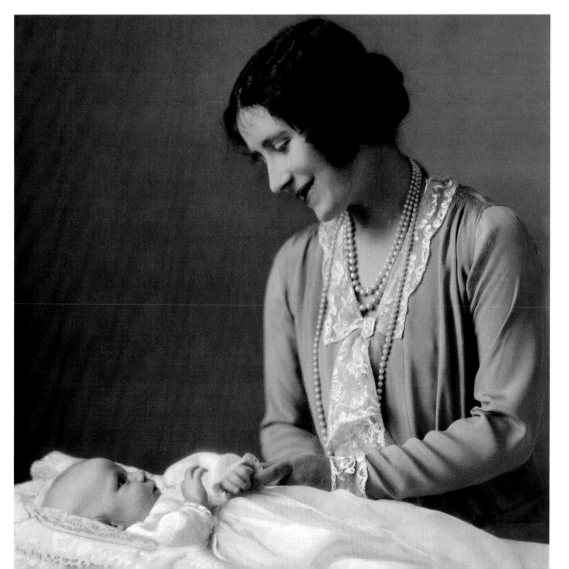

4 THE CRISIS THAT MADE A QUEEN

The meeting between handsome David, Prince of Wales, and Baltimore-born Wallis Simpson set in motion a chain of events which plunged the Monarchy into its most serious crisis of the 20th Century. The abdication drama of 1936 dramatically changed the lives of every one of its central characters – none more so than Elizabeth, Duchess of York.

She had already proved that Bertie had wisely chosen her as a wife, instilling in him a new confidence and becoming a truly popular member of the Royal Family in her own right. And as the abdication crisis unfolded, she was to demonstrate her single-minded determination to maintain the Family's dignity and position again and again. One of her

contemporaries memorably described her as 'a steel hand within a velvet glove.' And it is generally recognised that it was Elizabeth who did more than anyone to prop up the tottering monarchy during its most vulnerable days.

Wallis Simpson came into the Prince of Wales's life as a divorcee, having separated from her first husband to marry her lover Ernest Simpson – who split from his wife to wed her. Ernest's company sent him to work in Britain and the couple soon found themselves rubbing shoulders with Royalty. They joined the wide circle of friends enjoyed by the Prince, who had a reputation as a ladies' man – particularly among the wives of some of his chums.

[right] The Duke and Duchess of York visit a French Colonial exhibition in Paris in July 1931.

[top left] The young Princess Elizabeth exhibits an early interest in horses at the Richmond Royal Horse show in June 1934. The Duke and Duchess of York look on.

[bottom left] The Duchess of York opens the new buildings of Middlesex Hospital in May 1935.

[top near right] The Duchess of Windsor joins in the fun at a garden party in Regent's Park in June 1931.

[top far right] The Duke and Duchess of York during a visit to the Brussels Exhibition in July 1935.

[right] The Duchess of York at the opening of the Silver Jubilee building at the Heritage Craft School, Chailey in June 1936.

It wasn't long before David and Wallis fell for each other, with Ernest cast into the role of cuckolded husband – a role replayed 60 years later by Brigadier Andrew Parker Bowles as he lost his wife Camilla to Prince Charles. But while David was totally smitten with Wallis, she was having the opposite effect on other members of the Royal Family, including the Prince's mother Queen Mary – and the Duchess of York.

In 1935 David shocked every guest in Buckingham Palace's ballroom when he took Wallis to the Silver Jubilee celebrations of his father King George V. By

that time the King, a heavy smoker, was in poor health. All eyes turned on David and Wallis as they entered – and the American divorcee realised she had few friends, if any, in the assembly. In her memoirs she remembered the evening by writing: 'As David and I danced past the King and Queen, I thought I felt the King's eyes rest searchingly on me. Something in his look made me feel that all this graciousness and pageantry were but the glittering tip of an iceberg that extended down into unseen depths – depths filled with an icy menace for such as me.' As the King's health continued to deteriorate, it was clear he was becoming increasingly exasperated with his eldest son. By contrast, the stable family life exhibited by Bertie and Elizabeth had marked them out as his favourites. Somehow, he sensed his impending death would trigger a crisis and even confided in an old friend, Lady Algy Gordon-Lennox, by telling her: 'I pray to God that my eldest son will never marry and that nothing will come between Bertie and Lilibet and the throne.' How prophetic those words were to be in the coming dramatic months.

George died at Sandringham on January 20 1936, and David was proclaimed King Edward VIII. His first act as monarch was to telephone Wallis with the news. Then he quickly left Sandringham for a secret meeting with her at the Ritz Hotel in London, where

[top left] The Duke and Duchess of York appear on the balcony at Buckingham Palace during the Jubilee Celebrations for King George V and Queen Mary in May 1935.

[bottom left] The first published photograph of Edward VIII and Mrs Simpson, taken on a visit to Salzburg in August 1936. The photographer, Stanley Devon, had to hide the camera up his sleeve to take the shot. It was only later that the full significance of the picture was realised. Other, earlier, shots of Edward and Wallis Simpson were only published after the romance became known.

[top, far right] The King and Mrs Simpson on a trip to Dubrovnik during summer 1936.

[top, near right] The King and Wallis Simpson take a walk at Trogir, near Split, in Yugoslavia in August 1936.

[above, far right] The Prince of Wales on holiday in Biarritz in September 1935 goes for a trip on a pedal boat with Mrs Simpson.

[above, near right] The Prince of Wales returns to the Grand Hotel Villa d'Este after a yacht trip on Lake Como with Wallis in September 1934.

in 1999 Prince Charles and Camilla Parker Bowles were photographed for the first time as a couple.

The Duchess of York was horrified when she learned of David's rendezvous with the divorcee. In her eyes, the new King was showing a blatant disregard for his high office. Two days later there were more gasps when Wallis was at his side at the proclamation ceremony. Even at this early stage he was sending out signals that this was the woman he wanted to marry ... he wanted to make her Queen Wallis. The same day, Elizabeth travelled to Sandringham to comfort her grieving mother-in-law Queen Mary.

Six days later Wallis watched George V's funeral procession from St James's Palace. Sitting in a glass coach with Queen Mary was the woman who Wallis knew was going to cause her problems – the Duchess of York. The pair had met two years before at reception for the Duke of Kent. The meeting did not go well and as a close friend of the Duchess revealed: 'I am afraid Mrs Simpson went down badly with the Duchess from the word go.' Elizabeth was never discourteous but those who knew her could always tell when she did not care for someone, and she did not care for Wallis Simpson at all.

The frostiness continued when David took Wallis to the Yorks' Windsor home. The King wanted to show his brother his latest possession – a large American car. Wallis said in her memoirs: 'The Duchess of York's justly famous charm was highly evident. It was a pleasant hour, but I was left with the distinct impression that, while the Duke of York was sold on the American station wagon, the Duchess was not sold on David's other American interest.' Nor did the Duchess care for the racy set which surrounded David at his home, Fort Belvedere. The Yorks were a frequent topic of conversation there

> 'I am afraid Mrs Simpson went down badly with the Duchess from the word go.'

plainly see the way the wind was blowing and knew it was only a matter of time before it all came to a head.

The local paper printed two stories the following day. One referred to the King under the headline: 'His Majesty in Aberdeen – surprise visit in car to meet guests.' The other was of the hospital opening by the Yorks. While their popularity soared, Scotland never forgave the King for putting his private life ahead of his public duty. Days later, Queen Mary exploded in a rage when she glanced at a guest list for a Balmoral dinner and found Wallis's name appearing ahead of Bertie and Elizabeth.

It was to get worse for

[above] The Prince of Wales leaves Clarkson's the costumiers with Mrs Simpson in December 1935, a month before his accession to the throne and before news of the affair broke to the world.

[left] King Edward VIII and Mrs Simpson take a stroll on the west terrace of Balmoral Castle.

[right] The Duke and Duchess of Windsor with their pet dog take a break in Bermuda en route to the Bahamas, where the Duke became Governor-General in July 1940.

and Wallis took to poking fun at Elizabeth, dubbing her the 'dowdy duchess.' Wallis was also fond of mimicking Elizabeth as a goody two shoes, an image which she claimed was false and artificial. One night Elizabeth walked in unexpectedly just as Wallis was doing one of her impressions – and any hope of a rapprochement between the two was gone.

Elsewhere in Royal circles, courtiers were beginning to notice how Wallis was developing a powerful hold over the King, prompting one to quip: 'King Edward the Eighth and Mrs Simpson the Seven-Eighths.' The Yorks were also becoming increasingly concerned that the King was 'using' them while he pursued his affair with Wallis. One example came in September 1936 as David joined the couple in Scotland after a yachting holiday with Wallis and a group of friends. He asked the Yorks to take on one of his public engagements, an opening at Aberdeen Royal Infirmary, saying he was snowed under with work. Bertie and Elizabeth duly carried out the opening but while they were doing so, the King was spotted at Aberdeen railway station awaiting Wallis's arrival, sitting in his car wearing driving goggles and a scarf. The Yorks were furious. Elizabeth could now

the other Royals. None were aware that a few months earlier, David had struck an amazing deal with Wallis's husband Ernest. The husband agreed to put an end to their marriage by giving Wallis grounds for divorce, as long as David took 'good care' of her. Within weeks the King kept his side of the bargain by conferring a fortune on Wallis which meant she would have no financial worries for the rest of her life. The sum involved was £150,000 – equivalent to around £5 million now. Ernest also kept his word by inviting his mistress Mary Raffray over from America to stay with him, giving Wallis grounds for divorce.

The divorce action was heard on October 27 1936 in Ipswich, Suffolk – a venue chosen in preference to London in the hope that no one would take too much notice. Ironically, it was only the American people who knew of the relationship between David and Wallis. Unlike their modern-day counterparts, the British press paid strict reverence to the private lives of the Royals and kept the affair quiet. American newspapers went wild with speculation after the divorce hearing, with headlines including: 'King to marry "Wally" – Wedding next June" and 'King's Moll Reno'd in Wolsey's Home Town.' Behind the scenes

[right] The Duke and Duchess of Windsor at the Chateau de Cande in May 1937, a month before their wedding.

in Britain, the crisis was growing. David's aides and Prime Minister Stanley Baldwin were deeply concerned, and the King was questioned about his future plans almost daily. He remained clear and adamant – he would be King and Wallis would be his Queen. But Baldwin warned him of impending catastrophe and bluntly informed him that no constitutional manoeuvre would allow him to wed Wallis AND keep the throne. The King suggested a morganatic marriage, whereby the consort would have no privileges as Queen and any children from the union would not inherit the throne. This, too, was rejected. Eventually, David became so determined that he told Baldwin he was

> 'I am afraid there are going to be some great changes in our lives. We must take what is coming to us and make the best of it.'

prepared to give up the throne for the love of Wallis.

Soon afterwards the King's private secretary Alec Hardinge dashed to the Yorks' home to put them on notice to take over the throne as it was becoming clear that the King was about to cut and run. Bertie was shocked, panic-stricken and totally appalled at the idea of being King. He tried in vain to find out from his brother what was happening and pleaded with him to stay. But Elizabeth remained calm and told one of her trusted servants: 'I am afraid there are going to be some great changes in our lives. We must take what is coming to us and make the best of it.' On November 17, David called Bertie and told him he

[below] Newspaper headlines on the day of the Abdication. The press had maintained a silence about the discussions on the future of the throne, making the actual news of the King's Abdication all the more sensational.

intended to abdicate. And at long last the British press were forced to take notice and report. The whole Simpson scandal and the stories of her previous marriages were revealed, sparking a reaction among the people similar to that triggered by the revelations of how Prince Charles's affair with Camilla had destroyed his fairytale marriage to Diana.

Wallis immediately became a figure of hate. Stones were thrown through a neighbour's window in mistake for hers, and there were threatening letters and graffiti. (Camilla had bread rolls thrown at her at a supermarket, and received death threats).

On December 10 Bertie and his brothers, the Dukes of Gloucester and Kent, went to Fort Belvedere to witness the signing of the abdication. David sat at his unvarnished wooden desk, dipped his pen in an inkwell and tried to scribble his signature. There was a moment of dark humour as he declared: 'There is no ink in the damn pot!' But he borrowed a fountain

[below] King George VI, Queen Elizabeth, Princess Elizabeth and Princess Margaret photographed after the Coronation ceremony on 12th May 1937.

pen and signed: 'I Edward Eighth, of Great Britain, Ireland and the British Dominions beyond the seas, King Emperor of India, do hereby declare my irrevocable determination to renounce the Throne for Myself and My descendants and My desire that effect should be given to this instrument of Abdication immediately.' He stood and beckoned Bertie to take his chair. David had been king for just 326 days.

Twenty four hours later His Majesty's Declaration of Abdication Act received Edward VIII's own Royal Assent in the House of Lords. Bertie became King George VI and the Duchess of York became the Queen Consort and Empress of India.

David had one last goodbye to make to the nation that evening in his infamous broadcast. On Bertie's orders, he was introduced as His Royal Highness Prince Edward, then told the people: 'I have found it impossible to carry the heavy burden of responsibility and discharge my duties as King as I would wish to do without the help and support of the woman I love.' He added that Bertie had 'one matchless blessing, enjoyed by so many of you and not bestowed on me – a happy home with his wife and children.' At 2am the next morning, the destroyer *HMS Fury* sailed from Portsmouth without fanfare, taking the former sovereign into Wallis's arms – and into exile. Nine hours later the new King George VI addressed his Accession Council at St James's Palace to make this promise: 'With my wife and helpmate by my side, I take up the heavy task which lies before me. In it I look for support from all my peoples.' He also announced that from now on, his departed brother would be known as His Royal Highness the Duke of Windsor.

Bertie later showed his gratitude to Elizabeth for helping him through the crisis by bestowing on her the Order of the Garter, one of the highest and oldest orders of chivalry. He made the gift on his birthday, December 14, just as his father had honoured Queen Mary years before.

Ironically, Bertie's coronation was planned for May 12 1937 – the day David should have been crowned. There was some discussion by the Baldwin Government about whether the ceremony should be postponed, but Parliament decided: Same day – new King.

Although Britain had a new monarch, bitterness and resentment over Wallis Simpson lingered long within the walls of Buckingham Palace. She was squarely blamed for the abdication crisis by Elizabeth and Queen Mary. Mary felt that by taking up the throne, it was Bertie who had made the sacrifice, and

not David. And for years Elizabeth could not even bear to hear Wallis's name, often dismissing her as 'that woman.' Many years later, though, during lunches with friends, the Queen Mum claimed she never hated Wallis. She told former MP Woodrow Wyatt: 'Of course I was upset at the time, but I would never demean myself to hate her. I don't think I've ever hated anyone.' But there is little doubt her hand was behind Bertie's decision to deprive Wallis of the cherished HRH in front of her title, Duchess of Windsor, when she finally married David. Elizabeth persuaded Bertie it would send out all the wrong messages if a twice-divorced woman and the key player in David's abandonment of his kingdom was so honoured. David thought he had secured a promise of the HRH from Bertie, and flew into a rage. Wallis branded Elizabeth 'a clever and dangerous woman.' In turn, Elizabeth made it clear to Bertie that if he chose to receive his new sister-in-law, he could – but he would do so alone.

She was certain the crisis had caused serious damage to the Royal Family, damage that would have to be quickly repaired. Moreover, she declared herself opposed to any attempted return to Britain by the Windsors, fearing they could set up a rival court in which David would outshine the far less outgoing Bertie.

> The Cockney love affair with the new Queen had begun.

Elizabeth and Bertie began their rebuilding mission by touring London's East End, which was to feature so prominently in their lives. Crowds gave them an ecstatic reception, particularly at the People's Palace, a popular entertainment hall in Mile End Road. The Cockney love affair with the new Queen had begun. A few weeks later she made her first appearance at Wembley football stadium, presenting the FA Cup to Sunderland after they beat Preston North End in the final.

On the morning of Bertie's coronation, the King and Queen got an unexpected wake-up call at 3am. A technician was testing loudspeakers on Constitution Hill, showing that work was already under way for the pomp and ceremony that was about to unfold. More than five million people poured into London to cheer the Royal Couple – and this time the three-hour ceremony WAS broadcast on the wireless. The procession returned to Buckingham Palace, where the King, Queen, Queen Mary and Princesses Elizabeth and Margaret waved to the throng.

A month later, David and Wallis married in France in front of just 16 people. In London, BBC news bulletins dismissed the wedding in 55 words. The court circular the following morning ignored the event entirely, as did Prime Minister Neville

[above] April 1940: the Duchess of Windsor in her uniform as an officer of the French Women's Ambulance Corps attends a parade at Les Invalides, Paris. Less than seven weeks later the French capital had fallen to the Germans. The Windsors spent the rest of the war in the Bahamas; the Duke was appointed Governor in July 1940.

[above left] The Duke and Duchess of Windsor after their wedding on 3 June 1937. A Church of England ceremony was conducted by the Vicar of St Paul's Darlington and a French civil ceremony was presided over by the local French mayor.

Chamberlain when asked in the House of Commons whether a telegram of congratulation would be sent to the newlyweds.

It seemed relations between the Royals and the Windsors could plunge no lower, but they did when David and Wallis dropped a bombshell in September 1937 by revealing they were to visit the emerging Nazi Germany. While Bertie and Elizabeth fully supported Chamberlain's policy of appeasement in public, they privately deplored the rise of the fascist regime. And they felt a tour by the Windsors would no nothing but compromise the Monarchy, particularly as there had been rumours of David and Wallis having pro-German sympathies.

Again, Elizabeth laid the blame for the problem firmly at the feet of Wallis. Although the Windsors' visit was billed as a study of housing and working conditions, Elizabeth had no doubt they simply wanted to get back in the limelight.

The exiled couple went ahead with a 14-day tour,

meeting all the Nazi leaders including Hitler, with whom they had tea at his mountain retreat, Berchtesgaden. The German propaganda machine was not slow to react, and a picture of the couple and Hitler, sporting a huge swastika on his left sleeve, was wired around the world. Throughout the visit the pair were greeted with the words 'Heil Windsor' – and the Duke replied 'Heil Hitler.' He was even seen to give the Nazi salute. Gleeful Wallis discovered that in Germany, she WAS treated like a queen. Berlin ordered that she be addressed as Her Royal Highness the Duchess of Windsor. And she managed to make quite an impression on Hitler, who told aides: 'She would have made a good Queen.' Hitler also bemoaned the Abdication to one of his closest henchmen, Albert Speer. The Führer said: 'I am certain that through Edward permanent friendly relations with England could have been achieved. If he had stayed, everything would have been different. His Abdication was a severe loss for us.'

[below] Adolf Hitler greets the Duke and Duchess of Windsor at his mountain refuge in Berchtesgaden on their visit to Germany in September 1937. The Duke and Duchess had a two-hour interview with the Führer and took tea with him on a balcony overlooking the mountains.

[far left, top] The Queen, King George, and Princesses Elizabeth and Margaret inspect the Royal Company of Archers in the grounds of Holyroodhouse in July 1937.

[far left, middle] Queen Elizabeth inspects the London Scottish (Gordon Highlanders) in the grounds of Buckingham Palace in October 1937.

[far left, bottom] Queen Elizabeth and King George VI at the Knights of the Garter service at St George's Chapel, Windsor in June 1937. The King had bestowed the Order of the Garter on his wife the previous December and she has retained her connection with the order ever since.

[top left] Elizabeth pushes her beloved brother David and daughter Elizabeth (aged four) on a swing.

[left] Elizabeth and Bertie in miner's clothing visiting a colliery in County Durham in December 1936, just days before the Abdication. So suddenly did the crisis overtake the country that the news agency referred to the new king as 'King Albert I' and not by the actual regnal name he adopted, King George VI

[right] King George VI and Queen Elizabeth attending the Empire Day concert at the Albert Hall in May 1938.

5 'THE MOST DANGEROUS WOMAN IN EUROPE'

The storm clouds of war were already beginning to gather over Europe when the King and Queen undertook a state visit to France in July 1938. The Duke and Duchess of Windsor were living in Paris, but a month before the Royal tour they were bluntly ordered to get out of town by the British embassy. They grudgingly obeyed, taking a lease on a house in Cap d'Antibes on the French Riviera. If before they had the slightest doubt they were *persona non grata*, they could have none now.

The visit had originally been scheduled for June, but was put back by three weeks following the death of the Queen's mother, Countess Strathmore. In a bizarre twist of fate, the tragedy led to the Queen's first truly international triumph. She did not want to wear colourful clothes on the tour so soon after her mother's death, yet felt black robes of grief would be too austere. Her new designer Norman Hartnell came up with the solution when he suggested she wear white. Elizabeth did so to dazzling effect.

She won the heart of Paris and all its citizens, and there were only two voices of dissent – those of Wallis Simpson and Adolf Hitler. Wallis angrily surveyed Elizabeth's success from her Riviera retreat. Here was a woman she had dubbed the 'dowdy duchess' taking the fashion capital of the world by storm. And there was another bitter pill for the exiled Duchess to swallow, for just a few months earlier, Wallis Simpson's

name had been at the top of a list of the world's ten best-dressed women.

A newsreel of the Royal couple's last engagement of the tour, at Villers-Bretonneux, was angrily studied by Hitler. The Queen was at the King's side as he unveiled a memorial to the 11,000 Australians who fell in France during the Great War, and she spontaneously stepped forward and scattered on the ground an armful of poppies given to her earlier in the day by a schoolboy. The crowd was enthralled by such a moving gesture, but it infuriated Hitler. He turned to his aides and described the Queen as 'the most dangerous woman in Europe.' Hitler knew it was her opposition to the Windsors which had scuppered his plans to keep Britain out of a war with Germany, and could see also that here was an influential woman who had a natural ability to boost the morale of the masses. How right he was.

Another state visit quickly followed, this time to Canada and the USA. In Canada, crowds numbering more than half a million turned out to greet the couple. In Washington, a Texan Congressman complimented the Queen by saying: 'Cousin Elizabeth, you are a thousand times more pretty than your pictures.' And in New York, a staggering four million people took to the streets of Manhattan. Elizabeth was nominated as 'Woman of the Year' with a citation reading: 'Arriving in an aloof and critical country, she completely conquered it and accomplished this conquest by being her natural self.' Elizabeth

[above] The King and Queen on their official visit to Canada stop in the Rockies and chat to local people from the rear of the Royal train.

acknowledged the importance of the transatlantic tour in later years when she said: 'That tour made us. I mean, it made us, the King and I. It came at just the right time, particularly for us.' Despite their survival through the abdication crisis, and the success of their tours, Bertie and Elizabeth were still novices in their elevated Royal roles. But as Chamberlain's shuttle diplomacy failed, and Britain went to war against Nazi Germany, Elizabeth moved inexorably towards her finest hour.

Two events illustrated how this remarkable Queen was as crucial to Britain's war effort as any crack regiment in the front line. As Britons became gripped by the fear of air raids, Chamberlain suggested that the Royal Family should be evacuated to the safety of Canada. But in words that steeled the nation, Elizabeth told him: 'The Princesses would never leave without me, and I

'Arriving in an aloof and critical country, she completely conquered it and accomplished this conquest by being her natural self.'

[opposite] On board ship the Queen wraps up tight against the Atlantic winds on her way to her 1939 visit to Canada.

[above] The Queen chats with four Canadian Mounties, who acted as her personal bodyguards during the 1939 trip to the USA and Canada.

[left] A kilted King George VI with the Royal Family at a camp at Abergeldie Castle near Ballater in Scotland in August 1939.

[far left] An informal portrait of the King and Queen on board *The Empress of Australia*, the ship which carried them on their tour of Canada and the USA in 1939.

[left] For once at the other end of the camera lens, the Queen uses a cine camera to make a personal record of her voyage to the USA.

[below] September 1940: the King and Queen inspect bomb damage at Buckingham Palace. It was after this raid that the Queen said: 'At least now I can look the East End in the face.'

could never leave without the King, and the King will never leave.' The new, unofficial 'Minister for Morale,' as one American newspaper nicknamed her, had spoken.

A year into the war a German bomber pilot flew a daring raid down The Mall and dropped six bombs on Buckingham Palace. The King and Queen were in their offices at the time and were lucky to escape serious injury. But Elizabeth interpreted the raid as proof that the Germans, who were blitzing the East End, were making no distinction between Royalty and ordinary people, and she declared: 'At least now I can look the East End in the face.' It was a tense time. A unit from the Brigade of Guards mounted a round-the-clock watch on Princesses Elizabeth and Margaret, who were at Windsor Castle. And the King and Queen began target practice in the gardens of Buckingham Palace. Bertie used a .303 rifle and the Queen brandished a .38 revolver. As the Nazi hordes trampled over

> 'It does affect me seeing this terrible and senseless destruction. I think I mind it much more than being bombed myself.'

Europe, she insisted: 'I will not go down like all the others.' During the worst of the bombing the Royal couple visited East London to see the carnage and destruction for themselves. It meant a lot to the long-suffering East Enders – and once, as the couple trod through the ruins of a street, a local called out: 'Thank God for a good King,' To which George VI replied: 'Thank God for a good people.' Though their lives were as far removed from her as could be, Cockney women felt an instant affinity with the Queen. They crowded round her and yelled to each other: 'Ain't she lovely, ain't she just bloomin' lovely.' In turn, Elizabeth was full of admiration for their courage and determination. In a letter to Queen Mary, she wrote: 'I feel quite exhausted after seeing and hearing so much sadness, sorrow, heroism and magnificent spirit. The destruction is so awful and the people so wonderful – they deserve a better world.' In a second letter she revealed her own horror at the terrible sights which

69

confronted her. She said: 'The damage was ghastly. I really felt as if we were walking in a dead city when we walked down the little empty street. All the houses were evacuated and yet through the broken windows one saw all the poor little possessions, photographs, beds just as they were left. It does affect me seeing this terrible and senseless destruction. I think I mind it much more than being bombed myself.' On one occasion, she found an old lady weeping by a pile of rubble and was told the woman's pet terrier was crouching under the mound, too frightened to come out. The Queen, who had six dogs herself at the time, said: 'Leave it to me. I am rather good with dogs.' She knelt down and coaxed the shaking animal out into the daylight. Another time she took a baby from a mother whose arm had been injured by falling debris, and finished dressing the child.

In April 1941 a picture was taken in the East End showing the Queen exchanging smiles with a crowd. The caption read: 'Look at this photograph – the King and Queen, the cop, the kids, the crowd – and not a gloomy face among them!' She wore her normal stylish clothes on her visits, determined to maintain her elegance. She made it clear that uniforms were not for her. She had only worn one in her entire life, that of the Girl Guides, and joked that khaki was not her colour. She was challenged once when a woman asked her: 'Why are you wearing your best clothes in our

[opposite] February 1942: despite the war, life had to go on as normally as possible. Here at Buckingham Palace the Royal family celebrate the christening of Prince William of Gloucester, who is held by his mother Princess Alice, Duchess of Gloucester. By now the Queen had turned the Palace into the engine room of the war effort. She organised an army of volunteers making dressings for British troops.

[left] There is nothing like a good old cuppa, even if you are royal. Here the Queen enjoys a NAAFI break during one of her many morale boosting visits to a military base.

[opposite, far right] 1944: the Queen – on a morale boosting tour of the Land Girls – chats away to a group in Berkshire, near her wartime home of Windsor Castle. This was also the year that Princess Elizabeth joined the ATS.

[opposite, right] August 1943. The Queen riding in a pony and trap with the King and the two princesses on bicycles in the harvest fields at Sandringham.

bombed house?' The Queen replied calmly: 'If you came to my house, wouldn't you wear your best clothes?' She even perked up the brown box containing her gas mask by covering it with velvet.

Elizabeth put on another show of solidarity with the people by making sure rationing was the order of the day in Buckingham Palace, as it was across the nation. And she was appalled when a huge civic lunch was laid on for her during a visit to Lancashire. She rebuked the mayor for wasting money, telling him: 'We don't have any more food on the table at Buckingham Palace than is allowed to the ordinary householder according to the rations of the week.' The unfazed burgher replied: 'Ah well, you'll be glad of a bit of a do like this, then.' On another occasion the wartime Chancellor of the Exchequer,

Stafford Cripps, asked for an omelette during a Palace lunch. All the available eggs went into his dish, leaving young Princesses Elizabeth and Margaret to watch in horror as Cripps polished off their egg rations for the week. The Queen did not let on as the Princesses pulled faces behind his face as he tucked in.

[above] The visits by the Queen to the victims of the bombing raids by the Luftwaffe did more to raise morale than anything else. This visit to a bomb damaged day nursery in June 1944 was typical of the way she did all she could to support the war effort. It led to a US newspaper nicknaming her 'The Minister for Morale'.

[opposite] April 1940: an official photograph by Marcus Adams shows the closeness of the Queen, Elizabeth and Margaret – a closeness which survives to this day.

[left] Another example of her morale boosting visits came at the headquarters of the British Red Cross in 1939.

US president's wife Eleanor Roosevelt was surprised to discover during a 1942 visit that the Royal couple were sharing the same hardships as their people. She noted that Buckingham Palace was cold due to a lack of coal and that the King had ordered a line to be painted round the inside of his bath to ensure no more than the regulation five inches of water would be used.

Elizabeth made visits to arms factories, hospitals and casualty centres, and opened allotments which had defiantly been fashioned out of bomb sites. She made bandages and dressings for the Red Cross with her staff, while Bertie spent two evenings a week making ammunition. She gave a mother's blessing for Princess Elizabeth to join the Auxiliary Territorial Service just after her 16th birthday. The teenage Princess learned how to drive and change wheels, and during a visit to see her daughter in action the Queen proudly told one of her senior officers: 'Last night we had sparking plugs during the whole of dinner.' She autographed Lancaster Bombers, many of which later went down with their crews, and gently squeezed the arms of victims of Hitler's ferocious bombing campaign. She made a string of morale-boosting visits up and down the country, often sleeping overnight on the Royal train and prompting Home Secretary Herbert Morrison to declare that she was doing more than anyone to bolster the spirits of war-weary households. Her spontaneous actions needed no prompting from spin doctors or popularity polls, and she became a beacon of hope that Britain would eventually defeat the Nazi menace. Elizabeth never forgot her people – and to this day, they have never forgotten her.

Bertie regarded her as his trusted confidante and the pair worked together as a team devoid of petty jealousies over who was more popular than whom. What a pity, on reflection, that Charles and Diana did not learn from this lesson. In many ways Diana followed in the footsteps of Charles's grandmother with her charm, allure and caring nature. Yet Charles came to think of her as a rival. Like Elizabeth, Diana

[below] 1941: the King and Queen visit Aldershot to inspect a group of Canadian troops

had the ability, through her popularity, to make her husband more popular. Yet Charles saw her as a threat.

The Queen spread her wings by broadcasting a message of sympathy to the women of occupied France. It had a profound effect on those who heard it – and Hitler realised again that his initial fear of her was well-founded. Another broadcast to the women of America followed, thanking them for their behind-the-scenes help in the war effort. And at home, regard for her was soaring to unforeseen heights. Winston Churchill, now Prime Minister, noted: 'This war has drawn the throne and the people more closely together than was ever before recorded.' Victory in Europe was finally declared on May 8 1945. An ecstatic Britain celebrated and hundreds of thousands of people descended on the gates of Buckingham Palace. The Queen, King, the two Princesses and Churchill appeared on the balcony – and had to return several times to acknowledge the clamour from the heaving throng below. At the height of the frenzy the Princesses were allowed to slip out into the human tide, and were swept unrecognised down The Mall into Whitehall, where they ended up doing the conga through offices and hotels. Margaret stole a sailor's hat and was chased by him back to the Palace, though he never realised who she was. The young Elizabeth revealed in later years that the outing 'was one of the most memorable in my life.' The King spoke highly of his people – those who fought with the Allies and those who remained at home. And there was also a warm tribute to his wife. He said: 'I have done my best to discharge my Royal duty as the constitutional sovereign of a free people and in this task I have been unceasingly helped by the Queen, whose deep and active resolve for victory has comforted my heart never more than in our darkest hours.' In 1995 another massive crowd gathered outside the Palace to celebrate the 50th anniversary of the end of the war. Just as they had done in 1945 the Queen Mother and her daughters appeared on the balcony. Wartime forces' sweetheart Vera Lynn sang *The White Cliffs of Dover* … and the Queen Mum had a tear in her eye.

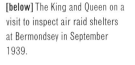

[below] The King and Queen on a visit to inspect air raid shelters at Bermondsey in September 1939.

[left] May 8, 1945: jubilant crowds gather outside the gates of Buckingham Palace on VE day, chanting 'We want the Queen'. The King and Queen along with Prime Minister Winston Churchill and the two Princesses, Elizabeth in ATS uniform and Margaret, acknowledge the cheers. Later the two princesses themselves slip away and join the throng below and join in the chanting for the King and Queen. The Queen prepares sandwiches for the return of the two teenagers and the King notes in his diary: 'Poor darlings, they have never had any fun yet.'

Chapter 5: 'THE MOST DANGEROUS WOMAN IN EUROPE'

6 TEARS, AN END AND A NEW BEGINNING

[left] In 1947 the Royal Family went on a tour of South Africa. The long sea voyage on *HMS Vanguard* there and back was seen as an ideal opportunity for George VI to recuperate. He was still exhausted after the war. It was the last time the family would go away together. They are seen relaxing on deck and also joining in a variety of activities including shooting [right]. In South Africa itself one Boer host told the Queen he could never forgive Britain for annexing his country. But she charmed him when she said: 'I know. We feel much the same way in Scotland.' Large crowds turned out to see the royals. Little did anyone know at the time the effect that the King's equerry, Group Captain Peter Townsend, was to have on the Royal Family with his courtship of Princess Margaret. He is seated in the front seat with Margaret behind [below left].

As the euphoria of victory in the Second World War died down, Britain set about the massive task of rebuilding. Winston Churchill, who achieved so much in the war years, was dumped in the General Election of 1945 and replaced by Labour's Clem Attlee. But of far more import to Elizabeth, the King was not a well man. Never the most natural of leaders, the stress and strain of the abdication crisis and then the war had taken a heavy toll on him.

There was happiness in the Royal household,

[left] During the 1947 trip to South Africa, the Queen, watched by Elizabeth and Margaret, tries to persuade a giant tortoise to eat a piece of lettuce .

[below left] The Queen arrives at Westminster Abbey for the wedding of her eldest daughter Elizabeth to Philip Mountbatten in 1947.

[below] The King and Queen at the wedding of Elizabeth and Philip.

however, over the engagement of Princess Elizabeth. During the war she had fallen for a handsome young naval lieutenant, Philip Mountbatten, nephew of Earl Mountbatten of Burma, and the couple announced they were to marry. The wedding was arranged for November 20 1947 at Westminster Abbey, giving the nation something to cheer after such a bleak time, just as Bertie and Elizabeth's marriage had done during the Depression.

A year later there was more excitement with the birth of Prince Charles. But by now Bertie was complaining of trouble with his legs. His doctors diagnosed a hardening of the arteries aggravated by smoking. His poor health meant more of his Royal duties were passed to the Queen and Princess Elizabeth, who gave birth to her second child, Anne, in 1950.

The following year the Queen was told Bertie had lung cancer. And in January 1952, the King looked drawn and haggard as he waved off Princess Elizabeth and Philip from Heathrow airport as they left for a five-month tour of Australia and New Zealand, via Kenya. A week later, Bertie died in his sleep at Sandringham after a day's shooting. He was 56.

Princess Elizabeth received the news that her father was dead, and she was Queen, after spending a night in a Kenyan tree house watching big game. She and

[right] April 1948: the King and Queen wave to the crowds as they celebrate their silver wedding anniversary. They are joined by Princess Elizabeth, the Duke of Gloucester, the Duchess of Gloucester, Queen Elizabeth, King George, Princess Margaret and Queen Mary.

[below far right] A gran for the first time: the Queen proudly holds baby Charles, born in November 1948.

[left] January 30,1952 The Queen and King on a night out to the theatre to watch the musical *South Pacific* at Drury Lane. Just six days later the King was dead.

[above] The funeral procession of George VI goes up the nave at St George's chapel, Windsor. Members of the royal family follow the coffin.

[left] February 11, 1952: the veiled figures of the new Queen Elizabeth II, Queen Elizabeth, now the Queen Mother, Queen Mary and Princess Margaret wait at the entrance of Westminster Hall where the King's remains are carried in for the lying-in-state.

Philip immediately returned home. Across the Atlantic the news was relayed to the Duke and Duchess of Windsor in their six-room apartment on the 28th floor of the Waldorf Towers in New York. David set sail for England the next day alone. The Queen Mum and Bertie's mother Queen Mary had both made it clear they were not prepared to tolerate Wallis's presence. Weeks after the funeral the Queen Mum still referred to Wallis as 'the woman who killed my husband.' To this day the Queen Mum still feels the loss of the King and never refers to him as the late King. Only a few years ago, as she tried to comfort a friend who had lost her husband, she said: 'Yes, it is

> Weeks after the funeral the Queen Mum still referred to Wallis as 'the woman who killed my husband.'

perfectly foul.' The friend asked if it got any better with time and the Queen Mother replied: 'It doesn't get any better but you get better at it.' Bertie was buried at St George's Chapel, Windsor, and for a time the Queen Mother retreated from public life, though with a warm public tribute from Winston Churchill ringing in her ears. He described her as 'that valiant woman, with the famous blood of Scotland in her veins, who sustained King George through all his toils and problems.' A lady-in-waiting has told how the Queen Mum was in such despair that she contemplated staying out of the spotlight forever. But wily Churchill, now restored as Prime Minister, spent

[below] May 13, 1952: the first public picture of the Queen Mother taken after the death of George VI. Here she is arriving back at London airport after a visit to Scotland. She wore black for a year. Friends told her what a brave face she was putting on, but she replied: 'Not in private.'

a time with her impressing on her that she still had an important role to play. It is what the King would have wanted, he said, and just as crucially, it was what the new Queen Elizabeth wanted. Soon, the Queen Mum adopted the title Queen Elizabeth, the Queen Mother, rejecting the one forced on her after the King's death, the Queen Dowager. To all at court, it was a sure sign that she did not intend to hide behind the walls of a Scottish castle for long. And three months later, she undertook her first public engagement since the King's death, bidding farewell to her regiment and that of her brothers, the Black Watch, as they left to fight in Korea.

Shortly before Queen Elizabeth's coronation on June 2 1953, Queen Mary died. Again the Duke of Windsor travelled to England alone for her funeral. Wallis could hardly attend a service for a woman who had refused to recognise her all her life. Neither of the

Windsors was invited to the coronation – and that, it seemed, was one problem solved. But another was looming … the doomed friendship between Princess Margaret and Group Captain Peter Townsend.

Townsend, a divorced war hero, had been an equerry to Bertie and was now head of the Queen Mother's household. Margaret had befriended him as a teenager and now that friendship had turned to love – and an intention to marry. It's hard to believe in these more enlightened days that such a relationship could cause such controversy simply because of Townsend's divorced status. But it did, to the extent that several Cabinet members threatened to resign if a marriage went ahead.

Margaret could not freely marry until she was aged 25. Until then, she required her sister the Queen's consent. A marriage would mean the loss of Royal

[below] The official photograph taken at Buckingham Palace after the coronation of Queen Elizabeth II on June 2, 1953. A very young Charles and Anne are in the foreground.

rank for her, but more importantly for those in Royal and Government circles, the prospect was seen as putting a huge strain on the Crown, the Church and the Commons.

It was the Queen Mum who stepped in with what she saw as a solution. Margaret would join her on a lengthy tour of Rhodesia, now Zimbabwe, while Townsend found himself relieved of his post at Clarence House and banished to the British embassy in Brussels. The hope was that the enforced separation would put an end to the

relationship, and there is little doubt the Queen Mum was against the match. Her strict views on the Royal requisites for marriage were well known – and duty to the nation was also of paramount importance.

It was during the visit to Rhodesia that one of the funniest incidents of any Royal tour happened. The Queen Mother and Margaret had visited an exhibition and were shown to their car by their host. They said their farewells, the door was closed and the car started slowly to move off. As the Queen Mum waved to crowds of well-wishers, the host

> Her strict views on the Royal requisites for marriage were well known — and duty to the nation was also of paramount importance.

[above] The Queen Mother and Princess Margaret arriving at the Coliseum Theatre, London for a performance of *Guys and Dolls* in August 1953. Just two months earlier Margaret, now a society beauty, had been forced to admit to her relationship with divorcee Group Captain Peter Townsend.

[right] The Queen Mother on a tour of New Zealand in 1958. She was now something of an international jet setter, taking on a large number of overseas tours. And she continued to be an able ambassador for Britain, with visits which also included Canada, the South Pacific and Australia .

in the door as it closed and he had almost choked as he was dragged along.

Back in Britain, in October 1955, Margaret and Townsend decided their love affair must end. Margaret chose Royal duty over love and issued a public statement revealing there would be no marriage. With yet another crisis over, the Queen Mum settled into her new role as elder stateswoman of the Royal Family … and grandmother.

Charles was always her favourite grandson, and she formed a strong bond with him which he has acknowledged on several occasions. Once, he said: 'Ever since I can remember, my grandmother has been a most wonderful example of fun, laughter and warmth and above all, exquisite taste in so many things. For me she has always been one of those extraordinarily rare people whose touch can turn everything to gold. She belongs to that priceless band of human beings whose greatest gift is to enhance life for others through her own effervescent enthusiasm for life.' Charles needed his gran's warmth. His relationship with his uncompromising father, Prince Philip, has always been difficult and the Queen has sometimes appeared cold towards her eldest son. There is

kept walking beside the car. The Queen Mum turned to Margaret and said: 'What a nice man, seeing us off so kindly.' The next time she looked, the car was moving faster but the man was still keeping pace with it and waving, though by now he was red-faced. The anxious Queen Mum told Margaret: 'If he is not careful he will give himself a heart attack.' Then suddenly she realised something was wrong and ordered the car to stop. The man's tie had been caught

'Ever since I can remember, my grandmother has been a most wonderful example of fun, laughter and warmth and above all, exquisite taste in so many things...'

no better example of this than when Charles was just five years old. He was taken to Waterloo station to

[right] The Queen Mum and her daughters lark about outside Princess Margaret's cottage. Even the corgis looked puzzled as the Margaret and her mother put buckets on their heads and the Queen carried a box.

[left] In all our years of covering the Royal Family we have never seen a picture where a lady has curtsied so low. This ballerina had been practising for hours to present a bouquet to the Queen Mother.

[right] The Queen Mum takes a trip on the river at Cambridge before watching the May races in 1960.

await the return of his parents from a Commonwealth tour. Seeing her son standing on the platform, the Queen walked over and shook him by the hand. But Charles shared a huge hug with his grandmother.

Ironically, Charles was at the centre of a similar incident in Canada more than 40 years later, and this time he found himself cast in the role of cool parent. It happened as he and Diana boarded the Royal Yacht *Britannia* to greet young sons William and Harry. Ever mindful of his duty, Charles stopped to shake hands with the ship's officers and crew, while Di ran along the deck with outstretched arms to hug the excited boys. Poor old Charles was branded – wrongly – an uncaring parent.

The Queen Mum is as indispensable a prop to him as his lover Camilla Parker Bowles. Few know that these days he forks out some £80,000 a year to help pay the wages of some of his gran's long-serving staff. The Queen Mum is out of touch with the costs of modern life and believes the somewhat meagre pay she offers is a living wage. Charles decided that rather than trouble her with the figures he would top up the salaries himself.

(The Queen Mother is reputedly in debt to the tune of about £4 million. But this does not take into account her possessions, some of which are of enormous value. She has at least one Monet painting hanging on her wall at Clarence House which is worth around £10 million. She receives £643,000 from the Civil List but the costs of keeping her in the style to which she has become accustomed far exceed this figure. It is believed the Queen dips into her own pocket to give her mother an extra £2 million).

Camilla is the only bone of contention between Charles and the Queen Mum, who because of her old-fashioned values frowns on the relationship. Like the Queen, she refuses to see Camilla or go to places where a meeting would be likely. She would also be deeply unhappy if Charles and Camilla were to marry in her lifetime.

Yet Charles often uses the Queen Mother's Birkhall home on the Balmoral estate to entertain friends,

[left] Dancing has always been a passion of the Queen Mum. Here she is at the Caledonian Ball in May 1959. giving a spirited performance of the 'Dashing White Sergeant.'

[below] The Queen Mother and Prince Andrew at Clarence House, London, on her 60th birthday.

[above] Generations apart but so alike in so many ways, these two women were both fashion icons of their day. Princess Diana and the Queen Mother have a chat in the Queen's box at the Derby in 1984. Although the Queen Mum tried to explain the finer points of the sport of Kings, Diana was never all that interested and stopped going to the Derby.

including Camilla. The Queen Mum knows this only too well, so Charles never asks her permission about who he can invite there, as this would place his gran in a difficult position. And despite Charles's adulterous relationship, the Queen Mum stayed firmly on his side when his marriage to Diana was torn apart.

When Charles first fell for the naive young Lady Diana Spencer, the Queen Mother and her close friend, Lady Ruth Fermoy, Diana's maternal grandmother, did nothing to discourage the pair from marrying. In the early days the Queen Mum saw Di as a breath of fresh air, just as she had been to the Royals in the 20s. But over the years, as it became painfully clear the marriage was little more than a sham, she came to regard Di as a 'silly girl' with little sense of duty.

> But over the years, as it became painfully clear the marriage was little more than a sham, she came to regard Di as a 'silly girl' with little sense of duty.

Though both the Queen Mum and Di were seen in their youth as new brooms sweeping the stuffy Palace corridors, the difference between the two is that the Queen Mother played by the Royal rules, whereas Di stepped outside them. In time Di became convinced the Queen Mother was her enemy, the strongest voice among those Royals who were trying to jettison her. In turn, the Queen Mum saw Diana's authorisation of Andrew Morton's biography *Diana: Her True Story* – which lifted the lid on her marriage woes – as a total betrayal of the Family.

She was further revolted by Diana's *Panorama* interview in which she admitted having a fling with Life Guards officer James Hewitt and, referring to Camilla, told reporter Martin Bashir: 'There were three of us in this marriage.' And, it has to be said, she

[above] Even on a rainy day the people need to see the royals, so the Queen Mum got hold of a transparent umbrella at Ascot races and gave a smile to the photographers as she walked to the paddock.

[top left] 1980, Sandringham Flower show, one of the Queen Mum's favourite days out, The Duchess of Kent shows Her Majesty a wicker basket that she has bought.

[left] The Queen Mum is very rarely seen without a hat and one of those occasions is when she goes to the opera at Covent Garden, London. We think the fur is fake – but don't bet your life on it.

[right] A favourite walking spot is Holcombe Beach in Norfolk, where, despite the weather, the Queen Mum used regularly to walk for a breath of fresh air. On this day it was hard to pick her out as she was so well wrapped up against the biting wind.

[below] Fly fishing is a skillful sport and a passion of the Queen Mum's. She is a master fisherman. Here at Birkhall Water on the Scottish estate on Royal Deeside she is casting for salmon. Sometimes the fish get their own back — which she has called 'the fish's revenge' — such as when she got a bone stuck in her throat.

was no more impressed with Charles's TV confession to his relationship with Mrs Parker Bowles. For the Queen Mum, there was too much washing of dirty linen in public.

Though the rift between the Queen Mum and Diana widened over many years, there were tell-tale clues early on. Di stayed at Clarence House on the night of her engagement to Charles and the night before their wedding in July 1981. Yet the tragic Princess moaned in later years: 'When I went to stay

at Clarence House I thought she was meant to help me, to teach me, but she did not do anything at all. I hardly saw her. She is not as she appears to be at all. She is tough and interfering and she has few feelings.' In the infamous Squidgygate tapes, Diana also revealed her lack of trust in her husband's grandmother. She said the Queen Mum 'gave me strange looks – sort of interest and pity mixed in one.' It was a view once shared by that other Royal outcast, Wallis Simpson. But finally, in 1972, the enmity between her and the

[above] The former Duchess of York bounces a future Duke of York, Prince Andrew, on her knee in this informal family shot at Balmoral in 1961

[right] At a 1967 memorial service for Queen Mary, the Queen Mother comes face to face with the Duchess of Windsor (far right) for the first time in over thirty years.

[overleaf left and above right]
The Pearly Queen. Like her hats,
the three strands of pearls that
she wears are another of the Queen
Mum's trademarks, as she showed
them off at the Sandringham
Flower show in 1979.

[overleaf below left] Falklands
Hero Prince Andrew, sporting a
full set of whiskers, is greeted by
the Queen Mother at Scrabster in
Scotland in August 1982.

[overleaf below right] The Queen
Mother and Princess Margaret
wave to the crowds at Royal Ascot,
which she never misses. All her
engagements at this time of year
centre around the week long
meeting.

[below right] The Duchess of
Windsor, flanked by Prince Philip,
walks veiled after her husband's
funeral. The Queen Mother
follows; her long-standing enmity
towards the Duchess cast aside
following the death of the Duke.

Queen Mum was cast aide following the death of the Duke of Windsor in Paris. His body was flown home to be buried at Frogmore, after which the mourners gathered at Windsor Castle. As well as being distraught, Wallis was clearly in a state of total disorientation, so the Queen Mum took her arm and gently guided her to a chair. 'I know how you feel,' she said quietly. 'I've been through it myself.' As Wallis's health deteriorated over the following years, the Queen Mum sent her a bouquet of flowers with the simple message: 'In friendship, Elizabeth.' And she was among the mourners when Wallis was buried next to David after her death just a few weeks before her 90th birthday in 1986. Also there were the Queen and Prince Philip, and Charles and Di.

Though the feud between the Royals and the Windsors was no more, there was a sting in the tail. Throughout their exile the Windsors had lived in Paris at 4 Route du Champ d'Entertainment, an imposing mansion standing in two-acre grounds on the Neuilly side of the Bois de Boulogne. It was given to them by the French government for a nominal rent of just £25 a year. Following Wallis's death, tycoon Mohamed

> As Wallis's health deteriorated over the following years, the Queen Mum sent her a bouquet of flowers with the simple message: 'In friendship, Elizabeth.'

Fayed, the Egyptian-born owner of Harrods and the Paris Ritz Hotel, bought the villa on a 50-year lease.

After the tragic 1997 car crash in Paris that killed both Princess Diana and his son Dodi, Fayed outrageously claimed the pair planned to marry and set up home in the mansion. He also insisted that Di had twice visited the building, the first time accompanied by an interior designer, and the second on August 30, the day before the crash, when she was said to have spent two hours viewing its rooms. Fayed's story was exposed as a sickening sham by *The Sun* when the newspaper revealed that Diana had visited the villa only once, for just 28 minutes on August 30.

[far left] Another visit to the Sandringham Flower show, where the crowds always turn out for her.

[near left] Ranger, one of the Queen Mum's two corgis, bows to his mistress as she celebrates her 88th birthday at Clarence House. The corgi seems to know only too well the royal hand that feeds him.

[below far left] The Queen Mum arrives at Clarence house after fulfilling one of her many royal engagements.

[below near left] Prince William joins the Queen and Queen Mother at the Christmas Day service at Sandringham in 1991.

[right] August 1988: the Queen Mother clutches a handmade card – one of the many presented to her by the growing army of fans who gather outside her Clarence House home in London each year.

[left] The Queen Mother, who is the only honorary female member of Lloyds of London arrives on a visit to the firm in April 1987. She was back again to switch on floodlights to start the insurance market's 300th birthday celebrations in February 1998. The new £200 million Lloyds building in Lime St was floodlit by 188 white, blue, and rose pink lights.

[right] The Queen Mother visits one of her favourite haunts – London's East End. Every time she made a visit to the area she was always given the warmest of welcomes. This visit in 1990 was no different.

[overleaf] 1988: the family gather outside Clarence House to celebrate another remarkable birthday. The Duke and Duchess of York, along with the Prince and Princess of Wales, Viscount Linley and Princess Margaret and the Queen, join the Queen Mum as she waves to the crowds. This line up has drastically changed in recent years with the break up of royal marriages.

7 'OH NO, DON'T TELL ME I HAVE DIED AGAIN'

[left] As elegant as always, the Queen Mum arrives at the Opera House in Covent Garden wearing a tiara.

The Queen Mother is perfectly aware that death is a fact of life, and is heavily involved in planning her final public event – her own funeral. It will take place at Westminster Abbey, where her Royal life began with her marriage in 1923. She does not find it disconcerting that she is drawing ever nearer that day, and is doggedly determined that even from beyond the grave she will be in full control of it.

Discreetly, senior royal aides have helped her with the arrangements for the funeral, which is code-named Operation Lyon. But, if you'll forgive the pun, she has taken on the lion's share. She has trawled over the details with the former Lord Chamberlain, the Earl of Airlie. She has helped choose the hymns and has inspected the procession route at least twice. She has also popped to the Abbey, where volunteers of the Ladies of St Faith, all needlework experts, can be found delicately repairing the Tudor roses on the Royal funeral pall.

Even in such at atmosphere of impending death, the Queen Mum's finely-tuned humour has helped put everyone at ease. On one visit she announced to the Abbey authorities: 'I am afraid that I don't awfully care for your candles. Do you mind if I bring my own?' The Queen Mother's attitude to death has always been one of acceptance. Once, in the 1960s,

[right] The Queen Mother watches a parade of London Taxi drivers in Horseguards Parade from an open top Land Rover. Every year the cabbies take underprivileged kids for a day out at the seaside.

she was at a concert at the Guildhall in King's Lynn, Norfolk, when a woman collapsed. A local policeman, Chief Superintendent Fred Calvert, rushed to the unconscious woman and carried her out of the hall. At the end of the concert, the Queen Mum asked him: 'How is the lady who collapsed, Mr Calvert?' Sadly, he replied that the poor woman had died, upon which the Royal guest said: 'Ah well, what a lovely way to go – listening to Chopin …' The Queen Mother has lived to see her own death wrongly announced THREE times. The first was in 1993, courtesy of an Australian radio station, after an amazing series of coincidences and misunderstandings. Wayne Hanson, an Australian TV videotape editor working for Sky News in London, was wandering to his desk when he saw newsreader Vivien Creegor wearing a black mourning dress amid a bank of monitors announcing that the Queen Mum had died.

What he didn't realise was that he was witnessing a Sky rehearsal for the grim day. He phoned his mother in Brisbane with the 'news' and she in turn called her local radio station, Radio New 822, telling them her son, who was in London, had just told her the Queen Mum had died. A reporter from the radio station checked it out by phoning Sky News, but unfortunately the call was taken by Wayne himself, who declared: 'Yes it's correct – it's on my screen.' The Brisbane station, believing it had a scoop in Australia and confident it had confirmed the report's accuracy, broadcast the sad news. The story

> 'Ah well, what a lovely way to go – listening to Chopin ...'

spread like a bushfire. Newsroom staff at Sydney radio station 2UE went live with 'unconfirmed reports' of the death, and Australian Prime Minister Paul Keating prepared to go on air with a message of condolence. Just before he did so, however, came frantic denials from Buckingham Palace. And instead of Mr Keating, the Governor General made a broadcast assuring Australia that the Queen Mum was still very much alive. Although she found the incident 'quite amusing,' poor Wayne had written his own death warrant as far as Sky was concerned. He was fired.

The following year Her Majesty found she had again taken her leave when a newsflash on BBC's Ceefax service reported: 'The death has been

[below left] The Queen Mother with her favourite grandson, Prince Charles at the Sandringham Flower Show in 1999. They arrived by coach.

[bottom left] The Queen Mother is helped from a carriage by a footman as she arrives at the Sandringham Flower show, watched by Prince Charles who could do nothing to assist his grandmother because he had a broken arm after a polo accident.

announced of Her Majesty the Queen Mother.' The flash appeared for less than a minute but it was enough to cause BBC switchboards to be jammed by upset viewers. Again, the flash was a rehearsal and had been transmitted in error. An apology was sent to Balmoral, where the Queen Mum was alive but not kicking. She was resting a sprained ankle after slipping on high heels.

By now she knew how American writer Mark Twain felt when he read of his demise in a newspaper, leading him to say: 'Reports of my death are grossly exaggerated.' But in January she suffered the same fate for a third time when news of her 'death' was posted on the Internet following days of rumour sparked when she failed to turn up at a Women's Institute meeting in the midst of a dangerous 'flu epidemic.

The Queen Mum is well aware that because of her advanced age, news organisations around the world have for years had tributes prepared for her death in case it happens just before their deadlines. And the day after her 80th birthday, she complained that reports in newspapers 'all read like obituaries.' But she mischievously turned the tables during a tour of Canada soon afterwards. Approaching Sun photographer Ken Lennox and another snapper at a cocktail reception, she made them choke on their drinks by saying with a smile: 'Ah gentlemen, have you come over to gather some new material for my

> 'The death has been announced of Her Majesty the Queen Mother.'

[below] An old Trooper herself, the Queen Mother here makes her way to Horse Guards Parade in London for the annual Trooping the Colour ceremony, a favourite with the tourists.

[left] One of the Queen Mum's most treasured honours is her membership of the ancient Order of the Garter, Britain's oldest order of chivalry. It was her husband George VI who made her a Garter Knight. Each year the knights walk in the Windsor Castle precincts to a service at St George's Chapel. She is normally escorted by her grandson Prince Charles, but lately she has taken a car to the service.

[right] Prince Charles offers his grandmother a steadying arm at a church service in St Paul's in 1995.

obituary?' Back home, she was tickled pink when she found out about an early-morning rehearsal of her funeral procession, and asked: 'May I make some suggestions?' Her biggest health scare was way back in 1966, when she had to have major abdominal surgery. But naturally, as she has moved into very old age, it is in the last 20 years that her health has been the subject of intense concern, comment and speculation. She has responded by steadfastly advising: 'Keep well away from doctors until you have no alternative.' And asked about the secret of her longevity, she replied: 'I love life – that's my secret. It is the exhilaration of others that keeps me going. Sometimes I feel drained – you do at my age – but excitement is good for me.' Despite such an active outlook, she has been dogged by problems. She was twice rushed to hospital after choking on fish bones – in 1982 and 1983 – but joked: 'After all these years of fishing, the fish are having their revenge.' In 1994 she was devastated when an injury to her foot, sustained when she slipped on gravel at Balmoral, forced her to miss a Remembrance Day service at London's Cenotaph.

In July 1995 she had an operation to remove a cataract from her left eye, which helped to ease her deteriorating sight. Before the surgery she pretended she could see perfectly well even though she couldn't, because she was too vain to wear spectacles in public. She had even been known to hold menus upside down while trying to keep up the charade.

A few months later she was back in hospital to have

[above] The Queen Mother at the Smithfield show in 1991 sports the badge of the Royal Smithfield Club.

[top left] The Queen Mother at Sandringham church chats to patients from the nearby Park House.

[left] The Queen Mother on another visit to the Sandringham Flower show in 1991 - an event which she rarely misses.

[right] On her 98th Birthday, the Queen Mother celebrates by attending a London theatre to watch the show *Oklahoma*.

[below] In her 99th year, the Queen Mother arrives at the re-opening of the Royal Opera House in London's Covent Garden.

[right] The Queen Mother joins actress Joanna Lumley, who played Patsy in TV favourite *Absolutely Fabulous*, at the Drury Lane Theatre in December 1988 for the unveiling of a statue to one of her closest friends, Sir Noel Coward

[left] In August 1991 five year old Kate Bush tugged the Queen Mother's arm at Sandringham and squealed 'Look at me,' dropping into a well rehearsed courtesy, bringing a huge smile to the Queen Mum's face. Her dad David Bush is a TV cameraman for Anglia TV and recorded every precious second for a nightly TV news programme and his own family archives.

[below] One of the few people the Queen Mother lets hold her arm is Fred Waite, former head gardener at Sandringham and now the chairman of the Sandringham Flower Show. Here, Fred escorted Her Majesty around the exhibits.

[right] The Queen Mother thanks a little boy who gave her flowers at Sandringham Church in 1998.

a hip replacement to banish creeping arthritis in her right hip. She had to endure several months of painful recovery. But the Queen reported that it had given her a new lease of life, and Royal officials said it 'clearly showed her determination to enjoy life for years to come.' Three years later, in January 1998, she had her left hip replaced after breaking it in a fall while watching horses at the Royal stud farm in Sandringham. A group of concerned locals gathered as she was helped into the car that took her to hospital. The Queen Mum, who was

> 'Don't worry – I have got my pearls to keep me warm.'

in the habit of attending Sandringham's annual flower show every July, noticed their frowns, reassured them that she was not about to meet her maker, and said: 'Don't worry, I shall be back in time for the flowers.' She kept the promise.

Prince Charles visited his gran in hospital after her op, and emerged to declare: 'She is completely and utterly indomitable. Absolutely unstoppable. I have no doubt she will be up and about doing eightsome reels again in no time.' The Queen Mum has always enjoyed dancing – and reportedly took the the floor briefly at last year's wedding reception for Prince Edward and Sophie Rhys-Jones at Windsor Castle.

These days the Queen Mum is visited daily by a district nurse who changes the bandages on ulcers on her legs. And the Queen maintains a close eye on her mother's health. She is particularly worried the Queen Mum might catch 'flu from guests invited to Royal homes and anyone unfortunate enough to exhibit the slightest sniffle or cough is politely asked to leave. A recent weekend visit to Sandringham by a well-known politician was disrupted when his wife complained of a sore throat. He stayed, but she left.

Once, as the Queen watched a Cheltenham horse race meeting on TV at Buckingham Palace, she spotted her mother at the course. It was bitterly cold but the Queen Mum was wearing just a three quarter length coat and a silk scarf. That evening the Queen phoned her and told her to she should wrap up more at her age. The Queen Mum replied: 'Don't worry –

[above] Prince William now a strapping 6ft 1" towers over his great grandmother as she rests during her 99th birthday celebrations.

[above right] Even in a raincoat the Queen Mother looks stylish, as she leaves church at Sandringham.

[left, above] The Queen Mother and Prince Charles share a joke at the Derby.

[left, below] Fashion is the key word at Ascot races and the Queen Mother and Princess Margaret lead the parade.

I have got my pearls to keep me warm.' There were more worries in January when the Queen Mother failed to turn up at a meeting of Sandringham's WI branch, of which she is president, to hear a talk by TV gardener Alan Titchmarsh. She had a cold – officially described as a 'sniffle' – and doctors told her to stay inside. But at the time a 'flu epidemic was sweeping Britain and old people were dying as their influenza developed into pneumonia. Panic swept the nation and *The Sun* and other newspapers were swamped with calls as fears about the Queen Mum's condition grew. The tide of rumour swept on to the Internet, and one website announced she had died.

It was not halted even when *The Sun* reported that she had been out to lunch with friends in the Sandringham area, and the rumours only subsided when she left Norfolk on January 31 to return to Clarence House. She always makes sure she is within striking distance of St George's Chapel in Windsor

on or around February 6, the anniversary of Bertie's death, so she can make a private visit to his burial place.

Despite her health restrictions, the Queen Mother is still an enormously active member of the Royal Family. In 1999 she undertook a staggering 114 public engagements. She has links with 350 organisations and charities, and her office is inundated with invitations to attend events. She also carries out a large number of private engagements which are not recorded in the official Court Circular.

She has largely ignored pleas from the Queen to slow down. But to help her get around, the Queen bought her a golf buggy in 1994, and replaced it in 1997 by a new model, a £3,500 American-made Medalist with a top speed of 15mph. The Queen kitted it out in her mother's horse racing colours, it has a specially-mounted plinth and gold tassel on the roof representing the jockey's cap, and its bonnet features a Royal crest. Driven by her loyal chauffeur Arthur Barty, and dubbed the Queen Mumobile by *The Sun*, the buggy has become a useful accessory on her birthday, when she still likes to meet crowds who gather outside Clarence House.

Though she rarely moans about anything, the Queen Mother once told her great friend Sir Hugh Casson, a former president of the Royal Academy of

[above] The newest member of the Royal family Sophie Rhys-Jones, now the Countess of Wessex after her marriage to Prince Edward, joins the rest of the family to celebrate the Queen Mother's 99th birthday.

[right] The Queen Mother with smiles as she arrives with Prince Charles to smell the roses at the Sandringham flower show.

[top left] Prince Harry helps his great grandmother down the steps in 1990 at Sandringham church after the Christmas day service.

[left] Princess Beatrice shivers from the cold in between her grandmother, the Queen and her great grandmother the Queen Mother at the Christmas day service at Sandringham in 1998

[far left] The Queen Mother after successful surgery to replace her hip attends Sandown races. The reason she is smiling is that she had a winner. Prince Charles said of the operation that it changed her life and said 'You can't stop her now.' It is rare for a woman of her age to have a hip replacement operation so late in life yet she has had two.

[below] The Duke of York and the Duke of Edinburgh defer to the Queen Mother as they leave by the Dean's House at St George's Chapel, Windsor Castle following an Easter service.

[left] Using a walking stick, the Queen Mother arrives for a very special lunch at London's Guildhall in November 1997 – to celebrate the Golden wedding anniversary of the Queen and Prince Philip. The anniversary day itself 24 hours saw the largest gathering of European monarchy in London since the Coronation. It included a thanksgiving service attended by 2,000 people at Westminster Abbey, where the Queen and Prince Philip exchanged their marriage vows 50 years ago.

[left] Returning from one of her favourite holiday destinations – Birkhall in Scotland, the Queen Mother comes down the steps of a royal flight.

[right] Each year without fail one of the first engagements to be pencilled into the Queen Mother's diary is the Smithfield show, where not only is she a keen visitor but she also exhibits her famous Aberdeen Angus cattle.

[preceding page] The Queen mum first used her golf buggy later dubbed the 'Queen Mumobile' at the Sandringham Flower Show. It was a present from her daughter the Queen and she hated it at first because it was an admission that she was getting old. But it has given her a new lease of life and on her 99th birthday, the latest version is decked out in her racing colours and brilliantly decorated to help her celebrate.

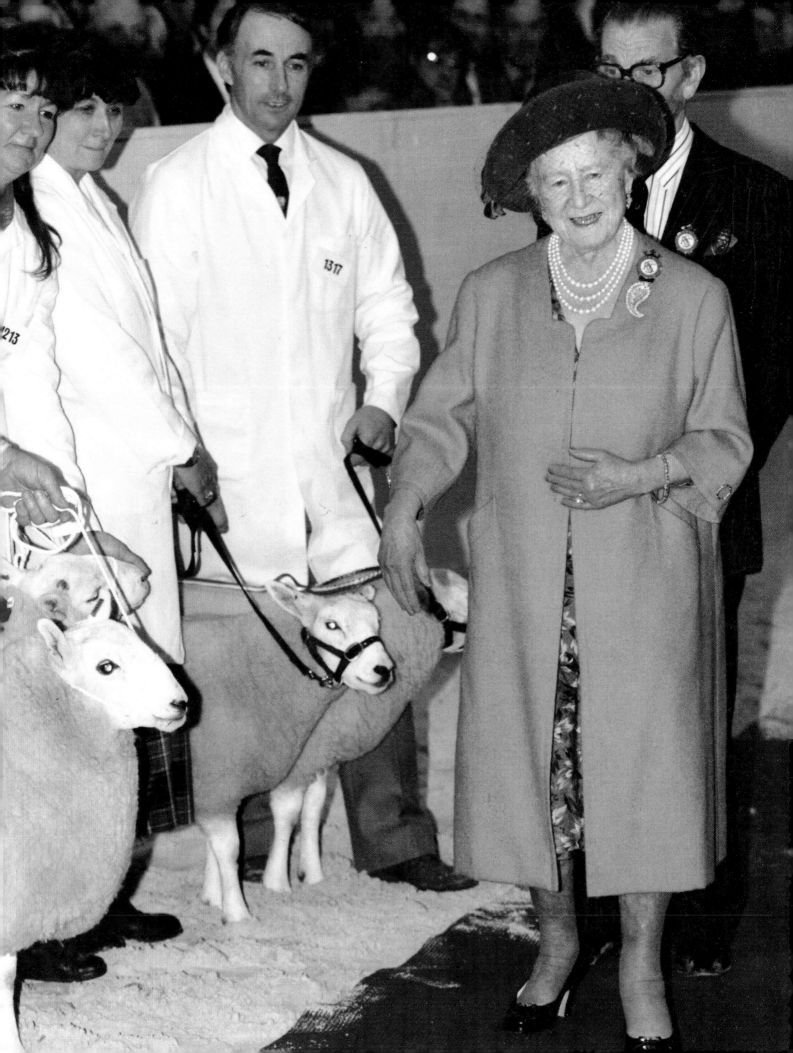

Art, that one of her regrets about old age was that it deprived her of one of her great passions – visiting the churches of France. She is a genuine Francophile and speaks fluent French. Often she sits and gossips in the language with the Queen and Princess Margaret, which usually drives Prince Philip to distraction – and out of the room.

Church-hopping and other physical activities may now be out of her reach. But the Queen Mother, who is among around five thousand 99-year-olds in Britain, still has one burning ambition … to celebrate her century with a telegram from her daughter! She will be no doubt be swamped with thousands of cards from well-wishers on the morning of August 4, but will be looking in particular for one white envelope with a distinctive Royal mark. Inside will be the same 6in by 8in card received by all 100-year-olds when they reach their ton-up milestone, featuring a picture taken at Sandringham of the Queen wearing a bright red dress, a string of pearls and a diamond brooch.

A personalised message reads: 'I am pleased to know that you are celebrating your 100th birthday. I send my congratulations and best wishes to you on such a special occasion.' It is signed Elizabeth R.

[left and right] Everywhere the Queen Mother goes, she is presented with many bouquets of flowers. Roses are her favourite flowers and she has had two roses named after her. One is called Elizabeth of Glamis and the other the Queen Mother Rose. Many of the flowers are sent to nursing homes and hospitals because she could not bear to see the flowers wasted. Her gardens at Royal Lodge, Windsor and Birkhall in Scotland are festooned with roses that her late husband King George VI planted with her.

[left] The reason the Queen Mum is Britain's favourite granny is because she always has a smile and wave for every body. She never has a bad day. Even if she is not feeling her best she puts on a regal display of affection. Even in her 99th year she carried out more than a hundred engagements, making her the oldest working royal ever.

[right] The Queen Mum at Sandringham in 1992.

8 HORSES, COURSES AND THE CHIT-CHAT CHAMP

[left] A young Prince William thoughtfully lends his great grandmother a hand as the royals leave an Easter service at St George's Chapel, Windsor.

There are few more daunting experiences than waiting to talk to a member of the Royal Family. And the Queen Mother, like many other members of 'The Firm,' understands what an ordeal it can be for those brought into the Royal presence. One trick she has adopted is to use one or two key phrases, which though fairly innocuous are designed to break the ice and get a conversation under way.

The Queen Mum is the British chit-chat champion. Her great friend Noel Coward once said her charm could turn the hardest hearts into

[top right] The Queen Mother looks at the new bronze statue of one of her closest friends Sir Noel Coward as it is unveiled at the Drury Lane Theatre in December 1998. She was captured deep in thought of her memories of the great man.

[right] Princess Margaret's children, Viscount Linley and Lady Sarah Chatto, try never to miss the Queen Mother's birthday lunch at Clarence House. With Princess Diana and the Queen they take a back seat as the Queen Mother holds centre stage.

'gibbering worshippers.' Three 'trigger' phrases which she used for years were 'Aren't the flowers lovely?' – a reference to the floral arrangements often made for Royal occasions – 'How are the children?' and 'Have you come far?' But the whistle was blown by the magazine *Woman's Own*, which ran a lengthy story disclosing what Royal Family members said as they walked along never-ending lines of subjects. After the article was published the editor of the time, Jane Reed, picked up the phone one morning to be met with a complaint from a somewhat plummy-voiced individual. He said he was speaking from the Lord Chamberlain's office and was rather annoyed – or at least the Queen Mother was rather annoyed – because she would no longer be able to use her key phrases.

The affair even spawned some light-hearted rivalry between two Labour MPs a few years ago as they waited to meet the Queen Mum at a St James's Palace reception. NATO chief Lord Robertson, then MP for the Scottish constituency of Hamilton South, was standing beside Robin Corbett, MP for Birmingham Erdington, and Mr Corbett's authoress wife Val. When Val pointed out that the Queen Mum was famous for her small talk, Mr Robertson said: 'I bet I can make her say something more.' Val laughed, 'You're on' and a bottle of champagne was placed on the wager.

Just then the Queen Mother drew near and shook Lord Robertson's hand. The minute she heard his broad Scottish accent, her face brightened and she

[left] The Queen Mother takes time to smell the roses during a visit to the Sandringham Flower show in 1979.

[above] After a visit to Sandringham church on her 96th birthday, dozens of children lined up to present flowers to Britain's favourite great grandmother.

dinner.' Others have spoken of treasured moments with the Queen Mum, just as thousands came forward after Diana was killed to talk about the Princess's common touch. One who met the Queen Mum was Bob White, a wartime sergeant in the 5th Battalion the King's (Liverpool) Regiment. He won the Military Medal for heroism during the Normandy landings but, because the war was still raging, King George sent him his gong with an apologetic message for being unable to present it to him personally.

It was always a source of disappointment to Bob that he missed his moment of glory at Buckingham Palace. And 53 years on, in 1997, his son Robert wrote to the Queen Mother, the colonel-in-chief of his old regiment, telling her the story. He received a letter almost by return post and a meeting was arranged at Clarence House. There, Bob chatted to the Queen Mum as they sat side by side on elegant gilt chairs, before she pinned his Military Medal on his chest. Robert, who was watching proudly, said afterwards: 'The Queen Mum was really marvellous ... she chatted away just like anyone's mum.' When the Queen Mother learned a few months later that Bob had died, she took comfort from the fact she had helped to brighten his last days.

She is just as much at ease out on the streets, meeting people with a style described by commentators as 'part Gainsborough Lady and part Pearly Queen.' In London when she was Queen, she asked one well-wisher: 'Where do you live?' In a broad Cockney accent, he replied: 'Back of 'Arrods, ma'am,

said: 'Oh do tell me how unemployment is in your area.' As Mr Robertson spelled out the high rate of joblessness Val was crestfallen, believing she had lost the bet. It didn't help when the Queen Mum, now at full chat, added: 'I do wish that little pockets of business could spring up here and there to employ more people.' As the conversation continued Mr Robertson caught Val's eye, happy in the knowledge that a bottle of bubbly was coming his way. But then the Queen Mum, turning to indicate huge bowls placed around the room, said: 'Aren't the flowers lovely?' Val claimed a draw and awarded Mr Robertson just a half-bottle of champagne.

Many are those who have been grateful for the Queen Mother's ability to put guests at their ease. One who arrived almost half an hour late for a private function had his humble apology interrupted when the Queen Mum told him: 'Don't worry, at least I've been able to watch the whole of *Dad's Army* before

'The Queen Mum was really marvellous ... she chatted away just like anyone's mum.'

[left] Who else could look this great at 99 but the Queen Mother? Having just spent two hours with her beautician, she radiates as she greets crowds outside Clarence House.

where do you live?' Referring to a famous old store near Buckingham Palace, she told him: 'Oh, back of Gorringes.' Nowadays, the Queen Mother's day starts with breakfast in her room, followed by a ritual that takes place at 11am no matter where she is or where her daughter the Queen is. A switchboard operator will ring, and when the Queen Mum picks up the phone she hears the words: 'Your Majesty? Her Majesty, Your Majesty.' Later there will be a consultation with her Private Secretary and if she has an engagement or lunch appointment she will call in her beautician Linda Thurston, who has held the Royal Warrant for 20 years. After a session normally lasting two hours, the Queen Mum is ready to face the world.

But there must also be time to read her favourite newspaper – the horse racing bible *The Sporting Life*. The Sport of Kings – and, clearly, Queens – has always held a magnetic fascination for the Queen Mum and her daughter. Both are passionate racegoers and racehorse owners, and relish studying runners, riders and form in the *Life*. Once, when the paper was halted by a strike, the publishers managed to print just two copies – one for the Queen and one for her mother.

In 1965 the Queen Mum had a bookmaker's 'blower' installed in Clarence House so she could hear race commentaries at the same time as bookies across the country. She arranges her diary around the racing calendar and likes nothing better than the camaraderie

[right] The Queen Mother, patron of National Hunt Racing, and Prince Charles attend Cheltenham Racing festival in 1979.

[overleaf left] Princess Margaret holds onto her hat as she and the Queen Mother arrive at Ascot races.

[overleaf right] The Princess of Wales and the Queen Mother delight racegoers as they travel together. The Queen mother wears her usual three strand pearl necklace, while Diana prefers a much more fashionable choker made of pearls with matching earrings.

[left] The Queen Mother with her winning race horse Braes of Mar at Sandown races.

found at the courses. She is still a regular visitor, with Ascot being a particular favourite. She refers to her horses as 'My darlings' and has pictures of them turned into table mats and drinks coasters, which she then hands out as presents.

She first became enchanted by the turf in 1949, when she took a half-share with her daughter in a horse called Monaveen. It went on to win several races and from then on she was hooked, developing more of an interest in steeplechasing than flat racing – the Queen's abiding passion. She has had around 500 winners as an owner but suffered her biggest disappointment when Devon Loch collapsed 50 yards from the line while romping home to certain victory in the 1956 Grand National. Jockey Dick Francis, later to become a celebrated thriller writer, was devastated, but the Queen Mother tried to console him – and herself – by saying: 'That's racing, I suppose.' It is rare for the Queen Mum to be distracted at a racecourse but her close friend Woodrow Wyatt remembered one famous occasion. In his diaries, he told of the time he was invited to tea with the Queen and Queen Mother during Royal Ascot in 1989. When he arrived at the Royal Box he

was politely but curtly greeted by the Queen, then settled down for a chat with the Queen Mum. As they talked on, they became oblivious to everything around them – and suddenly realised everyone else had left the Box. The Queen Mum turned to Wyatt and asked him to join her in watching the big race, leading him to the large chairs at the front of the Box. Thinking the race was about to start, the Queen Mum put her binoculars to her eyes, but neither she nor Wyatt could spot any horses.

Both were mystified, particularly as on a television behind them they could plainly see the race under way, and Wyatt was moved to exclaim: 'How very odd.' Moments later the Queen arrived and asked her mother what she was doing with the binoculars, to which the Queen Mum replied that she was trying to watch the race. The Queen, her face already spreading into a smile, said: 'But it's finished – that's a replay on the television.' With that, the Queen's smile turned to laughter. Wyatt said he had never seen her laugh so much. Unruffled, the Queen Mum just looked at her daughter and said: 'We are not very good at the flat racing, we prefer the jumping.' She is also gloriously politically incorrect and many of her observations would have landed lesser mortals in the soup. Although fond of individual Germans she does not like them as a race and habitually refers to them as the Huns – seemingly ignoring the fact that German blood runs through the Royal Family's veins. She has strong views on almost every topic and freely expresses them in private, caring not a jot whether her view would offend its intended target.

Aides have revealed she has little time for the European Union and loathes the idea of the Euro single currency. She believes Britain has a wonderful history which she does not want subsumed in a European federation. It is her belief that the Euro is a potentially fatal step towards such a perceived disaster. She is in favour of capital punishment and stiff prison sentences for criminals and is against immigration and the ordination of women priests. Her favourite Prime Minister was Margaret Thatcher and she adored Mrs T's husband Denis, who she described as 'such a sensible man.' She developed a particular dislike of Ugandan dictator Idi Amin, left-wing firebrand Tony Benn and one-time U.S. President Jimmy Carter, and there have been times after dinner when she has raised her glass in a mocking toast to one or the other. Carter was crossed off her lunch guest list when he kissed her a little too warmly, leading her to declare: 'Nobody has kissed me on the lips since my husband died.' By contrast, she allowed Italian opera star Luciano Pavarotti to get somewhat over-familiar. He got carried away after performing before her at the Royal Opera House in Covent Garden. Instead of taking her hand and bowing, he kissed it and then proceeded to smooch on up to her elbow. The Queen Mum giggled and said: 'Please, can you do that again?' For many years she has been known as one of society's premier hostesses. And scores of her guests – young as well as old – have struggled to keep pace with her when it comes to enjoying a stiff

> 'Nobody has kissed me on the lips since my husband died.'

[below] Overexcited Irishman Michael Dailey couldn't help himself when he grabbed the Queen Mother and planted a smacker on her cheek. It was at Cheltenham Races in March 1987. His horse had just won one of the première races and as the Queen Mum presented him with his trophy, he was so happy he just put his arm around her and kissed her.

[above] If anyone ever had any doubt of the passion the royals have for horse racing, it was dismissed in the famous TV documentary *Elizabeth*. Here TV cameraman Philip Bonham-Carter records the Queen's delight having picked the winning horse at the Derby. Her Majesty had drawn the horse in the Royal Family's own sweepstake.

[left] The Queen Mum, the Queen and one of the royal corgis share a joke at the Badminton horse trials.

drink. The Queen Mum's reputation when it comes to a drop of the hard stuff is legendary. She likes strong Martinis, gin and Dubonnets, and   of course champagne. Often, she tells staff who are pouring her a drink, 'Just a splash' and then adds: 'Just a splash more.' Despite her age, and despite the fact that it is her daughter who is Queen, she retains an enormous influence over the Royals, and few courtiers or members of the family are brave enough to take her

> Often, she tells staff who are pouring her a drink, 'Just a splash' and then adds: 'Just a splash more.'

on. But in recent years, her insistence on tradition has sometimes met with defeat as the Royal household has been forced to modernise. She was against the Queen's decision to pay tax and the loss of the Royal yacht *Britannia*, for example.

The Queen still openly refers to her as 'mummy' and many observers are slightly taken aback when they hear the Queen talking to her mother like an admonished child by saying such things as: 'Oh, all right, mummy.' But only once have mother and daughter appeared to exchange angry words in public. It happened as they went into a theatre, when the Queen Mum was heard to bark: 'Just who do you think you are?' Back came the inevitable reply: 'I'm the Queen, mummy, the Queen.' Newspapers have many reasons to thank the Queen Mum, for over the years she has given us some marvellous stories and pictures. Some of the most memorable photos were taken while she was pursuing another of her favourite pastimes, fishing.

She became an accomplished angler and could often be found up to her waist in the River Dee, which runs through the Balmoral estate. And although she once landed a 26lb salmon, her biggest catch, she was no different from any other angler in the world, often bemoaning 'the one that got away.' Once at her fishing hut near the Dee, where she still entertains friends, she was seen with nothing to show for a morning's line-casting. Still wearing her waders and loop round her neck that supported a stick she prodded for safe ground, she stood with arms outstretched as wide as possible to explain how big her catch would have been …. had it just taken the bait.

It was while fishing in 1980 that she allowed photographer Ken Lennox to come close so he could get some superb action shots. When she felt he had enough, she gave him a friendly wave – the sign for him to depart with his pictures. As Ken says: 'She was always a lady.'

[right] Every fisherman tells a tall story about the one that got away and the Queen Mother is no exception. Here at her fishing lodge on the banks of the River Dee at Birkhall, she explains to her guests just how big the salmon was who escaped all her best efforts to land him.

Picture Credits

The majority of the photos in this book were taken by Arthur Edwards, Royal Photographer of *The Sun*. Many of the photographs illustrating the earlier part of the Queen Mum's life have been taken from the archives of *The Times* newspaper (listed as TNL below). All reasonable efforts have been made by News Group Newspapers to trace the copyright holders of the photographs contained in this publication. In the event that a copyright holder of a photograph has not been traced but comes forward after the publication of this book, News Group Newspapers will endeavour to rectify the position at the earliest opportunity. The publishers would like to thank the following for their permission to reproduce pictures published in this book.

Front cover *The Sun*: Arthur Edwards; p. 3 (far left) Topham Picturepoint (centre) Press Association (centre right, far right) *The Sun*: Arthur Edwards; p. 6 (top) Rex Features (middle) Topham Picturepoint (bottom) TNL; p. 7 (top, upper middle) TNL (lower middle, bottom) *The Sun*: Arthur Edwards; p. 9-11 *The Sun*: Arthur Edwards; p. 12 TNL; p. 13 *The Sun*: Arthur Edwards; p. 14 *The Sun*; p. 16 *The Sun*: Arthur Edwards; p.18 Ron Bell; p.19-22 *The Sun*: Arthur Edwards; p. 23 *The Sun*: P Simpson; p. 24 St Paul's Walden Bury ; p. 25 (bottom) Popperfoto; p. 26 (left) Rex Features, 27 (left) Rex Features; p. 27 (right) St Paul's Walden Bury; p. 29 Rex Features; p. 30 Topham Picturepoint; p. 31 National Portrait Gallery; p. 33 (bottom right) Rex Features; p. 34 (top) Rex Features; p. 34 (bottom) St Paul's Walden Bury; p. 36 TNL; p. 38 -9 TNL; p. 41 Topham Picturepoint; p. 42-3 TNL; p. 44 Basssano & Vandyk/National Portrait Gallery; p. 45 (top right and bottom) TNL; p. 45 (top left) Central Press; p. 46 TNL; p. 47 (bottom) TNL; p. 48 TNL; p. 49 (top) TNL; p. 49 (bottom) Popperfoto; p. 50 Press Association; p. 51-4 (top) TNL; p. 55 (bottom) Daily Sketch/Stanley Devon; p. 55 (top left) Daily Sketch; (bottom right) Associated Press; p. 59 TNL; p. 60 (right) Daily Sketch; p. 62 (top left, centre left, bottom left) TNL; (top right) Rex Features; (bottom right) Fox Photos; p. 63 TNL; p. 64 Camera Press/Cecil Beaton; p. 65-75 TNL; p. 78-80 TNL; p. 81 (top, bottom left) TNL; p. 81 (bottom right) Press Association; p. 82-5 TNL; p. 87 TNL; p. 88 Ken Lennox; p. 89 (bottom) Photographic News Agency; p. 90 TNL; p. 91-93 (top) *The Sun*: Arthur Edwards; p. 93 (bottom) Ken Lennox; p. 94 TN; p. 95 (right) TNL; p. 96-99 *The Sun*: Arthur Edwards; p. 100 London Daily News; p. 101-106 *The Sun*: Arthur Edwards; p. 107 PA News; p. 108-133 *The Sun*: Arthur Edwards; p. 133 PA News/John Stilwell; p. 134-141 *The Sun*: Arthur Edwards; p. 142-3 Ken Lennox; Back cover National Portrait Gallery